Mexico/USA

This issue is dedicated to
Swannie (Jill) Zink Tarbel,
1924-2009,
a champion who supported with vigor
the many causes that stirred her heart and mind.

Nimroð International Journal

Mexico/USA

Nimroð International Journal IS INDEXED IN HUMANITIES INTERNATIONAL COMPLETE

The University of Tulsa is an equal opportunity/affirmative action institution. For EEO/AA information, contact the Office of Legal Compliance at (918) 631-2602; for disability accommodations, contact Dr. Jane Corso at (918) 631-2315.

ISBN: 0-9794967-3-X

ISSN: 0029-053X

Volume 52, Number 2

Spring/Summer 2009

THE UNIVERSITY OF TULSA
TULSA, OKLAHOMA

ACKNOWLEDGEMENTS

This issue of *Nimrod* is funded by donations, subscriptions, and sales. *Nimrod* and The University of Tulsa acknowledge with gratitude the many individuals and organizations that support *Nimrod*'s publication, annual prize, and outreach programs: *Nimrod*'s Advisory and Editorial Boards; and *Nimrod*'s Angels, Benefactors, Donors, and Patrons.

ANGEL
($1,000+)

Margery Bird, Ivy & Joseph Dempsey, Marion & Bill Elson, Joan Flint, The Herbert & Roseline Gussman Foundation, Bruce Kline, Edwynne & George Krumme, Susan & Robert Mase, Donna O'Rourke & Tom Twomey, Mary Lee Townsend & Burt Holmes, Ann Daniel Stone, Randi & Fred Wightman, The John Steele Zink Foundation

BENEFACTOR
($500+)

Cynthia Gustavson, Evelyn Hatfield, Thomas Matson, Ruth K. Nelson, Andrea Schlanger, Joy Whitman, Josephine & Thomas Winters, Rachel Zebrowski

DONOR
($100+)

Teresa & Alex Adwan, Margaret Audrain, Harvey Blumenthal, Colleen Boucher, Harry Cramton, Katherine & John Coyle, Dianne & Dick Dericks, Kay & F. Daniel Duffy, Nancy & Ray Feldman, Sherri Goodall, Helen Jo Hardwick, Ellen Hartman, Ben Henneke, Mary & Douglas Inhofe, Carol Johnson, Sam & Liz Joyner, Inge Kahn, The Kerr Foundation, William Kellough, Marjorie & David Kroll, Lydia Kronfeld, Robert Lafortune, Sandra & Dobie Langenkamp, Maria Lyda, Roberta & Dan Marder, James McGill, Carol McGraw, Melvin Moran, Catherine Gammie Nielsen, Rita Newman, Oklahoma Visual Arts Coalition, Nancy & Tom Payne, Lisa Ransom, Kate Reeves, Patricia Rohleder, R. A. Searcy, Joan Seay, Diane & James Seebass, Dorothy & Michael Tramontana, Sarah Theobald-Hall, Fran & Bruce Tibbetts, Renata & Sven Treitel, Melissa & Mark Weiss, Marlene Wetzel, Penny Williams, Martin Wing

PATRON
($50+)

M. E. & Helen Arnold, Phyllis Collier, Jean Curry, Patricia Eaton, Susan & William Flynn, Carolyn Gardner, Marilyn Inhofe, Olivia Marino, Geraldine McLoud, John Mitchell, Si & James Murray, Maynard Ungerman, Maralee Waidner, Krista & John Waldron, Ruth Weston

TABLE OF CONTENTS

OVER-THE-TRANSOM SECTION

Editor's Note:
The Real and the Romanticized Mexico/USA

In this selective feature on Mexico, *Nimrod* once again fulfills its mission of discovery. In two previous issues devoted to Latin American culture (Fall 1973, Spring 1983), *Nimrod* published Octavio Paz, Isabelle Fraire, Marco Antonio Montes de Oca, and other distinguished Mexican writers. Today (Spring 2009) we introduce new or little known Mexican writers in translation and, as often as space permits, in their original Spanish, Mixtec, or Zapotec (Margarito Cuéllar, Pedro Serrano, Pancho Nácar, Jorge Granados, and others). Often the authors' names sound misleading (Seidman, Kort, Kreiter, Raab), revealing the complexity of what it means to be Mexican and American. Several selections represent native English speakers writing about Mexico. At the same time, there are Chicano writers refreshing the English of their present homeland with the Spanish of their roots. As John Surowiecki says in his poem, echoing Kafka, "Nothing lives without changing into something else."

Those transformations, through translation or inclusiveness, reveal, in this gathering of fiction, poetry, and essay, the romantic vision of Americans who still see Mexico, despite its bad publicity, as a timeless land of bougainvilleas and bright birds, of soul-sustaining story and life-explaining myth. There is, inevitably, in this quest for life and change, the parallel dream of Mexicans who envision the United States as a land where, as my Russian great-grandmother said, the streets are paved with gold, gold so alluring that they are willing to walk barefoot to find it, as in María Victoria's "A La Fuerza."

For here too, in this issue, is the reality: the hard, often repeated, sometimes "endless" journey; the placement, temporary or permanent, in boxes, walled enclaves, sub-standard lots. And, of course, there are the gratuitous acts of violence on both sides of the border and still the gardens and the cities tended and then rising out of the rubble. This life is never orderly, never tame, never prescribed —who comes back, who dies, who lives in joy and abundance of spirit. When we ask of a Mexican walking down our streets, "Where do you come from?" he or she might appropriately state, as recent archaeological and cultural findings suggest, "right here, Utah" perhaps.

Birds flit through this issue: the wren, the owl, the goldfinch, the canary, the tiny ones "waiting patiently on a wire," and the archetypal plumed serpent who doesn't "flit" but rather seems to grow from the stone of ancient Mayan pyramids and contemporary paintings and literature or soar into nightmare. The birds connect the Mexican feature section to the "over-the-transom" section of this issue (works submitted throughout the year with no particular theme in mind).

And here, in this section, are once again the flocks of gifted writers who settle on our land and then push off and fly free from the firm ground that *Nimrod* provides.

Michelle Firment Reid, *I Left You in the Mood*, mixed media on paper

Francisco Toledo, drypoint

Tao de mí

Vamos a no entender nada
de lo que aquí sucede

a pedirle al sentido que regrese
por donde vino
y como llegó:
de la nada de ningún dios

a insinuar, no a decir
que nada tiene hondura
nada tiene precio
más alto
que subir
subir
para ver lo invisible.

My Tao

Let's understand nothing
of what's going on here

let's ask meaning to go back
where it came from
the way it came:
from the nothingness of no god

let's insinuate but not say
that nothing has depth
nothing has a higher price
than rising
and rising
to see
what can't be seen.

Translated from the Spanish by Dan Bellm

Enigma de señales

En Viena un día nublado
en un muro gris de un palacio
donde yacen
      el penacho de Moctezuma
y el escudo de Ahuítzotl
vi a una mariposa girar
sus alas gris y escarlata.
No entendí su sistema de señales
y fue tan perfecto su silencio
que los automóviles se ahogaron
en la luz de sus cristales.

Enigma of Signals

In Vienna on a cloudy day
on the gray wall of a palace
wherein lie
      the feather crown of Moctezuma
      & the shield of Ahuitzotl
I saw a butterfly wave
its gray & scarlet wings.
I did not understand its system of signals
& so perfect was its silence
that the automobiles drowned
in the crystals of its light.

Translated from the Spanish by the author

Gerald Cournoyer, *Black Mesa Morning*, acrylic on canvas

Canarios / Canaries

The most important thing is the cage, two yellow terrors inside, two fears at my mercy to add to the ones I already carry inside. They breathe with me, they see, listen, I'm certain they listen because when I put on a record, they stretch their necks, alert. In the morning, you have to uncover them quickly, clean their cage, change their water, replace their earthly nourishment. Then the grass must be stored in a big bowl of water, like watercress, if not, it dries out; the birdseed, the minute bowls, the little round splinterless stick shaped like a perch that they stand on, the banana, the apple, whatever I have on hand. No one's ever given me a stick I can rest my fears on.

They tremble their yellow trembling, they move their little heads this way and that; standing in front of them I must be an immense mass that blocks the sun, an opaque gelatin, a semolina flan to feed a giant, someone who occupies a disproportionate amount of space that doesn't belong to her. They make me hate my big round bear-like shadow that terrorizes.

The cage is what's heavy, they're so light, they have eyes of nothing, jumping birdseed, a micron of black matter and, nevertheless, they throw looks like darts. I shouldn't let them intimidate me.

They're perceptive; they turn their heads before I can turn my greasy human head, my white face that hangs on a butcher's shop hook since they arrived. I try not to think about them. Yesterday they weren't part of my daily grind, today I can pretend that I'm still free, but the cage is there.

The first night, I cover it with a towel and hang it next to the enormous wooden seagull that has to be dusted because we all forget to make it fly. The second night, I look for another spot. The cat lies in wait, he tenses his body, stretches his neck, his body stays rigid like a wire all day, his nature frustrated to the tip of each of his black hairs. I run him off. He returns. I run him off again. He doesn't understand. I no longer have patience for those who don't understand.

The second night, I pick my bathroom, it's safer. It has a good door. At sundown, I cover them and they huddle together in a ball of feathers. When it gets dark, I can't go into the bathroom because if I turn on the light I'll interrupt their sleep. What must they think about the immense mass that brushes her teeth to the thunder of pipes? What must they think about the roar of water from the last flush of the toilet? What must they think about the pajamas I've been wearing for three days, ridiculously pink and oversized, with blue patches? I must look like the glittery felt dashboard of a taxi to them. And now, what do I do? Dear God, it's awful being a man. Or a woman. Human, whatever. Occupying so much space. A thousand times more than they do. I sleep uneasy: every once in a while I get up and I slide my hand through a crack beneath the towel to make sure they're still in there huddled together in a feathery ball, their heads nestled inside their shoulders. Unlike me, they sleep embraced, like lovers.

The next morning, I take them back out to the terrace, to the sun, the air, to the possible visit of other birds. They don't sing, they emit a few chirps, very thin, weak, sad. They don't like the house. At noon, my daughter notices:

—One got away.

—How?

—Through the bars in the door.

—Didn't I tell you to put the door against the wall?

—Doors aren't supposed to face the wall, doors open to the street.

—You were supposed to hang the cage with the door facing the wall.

—Oh, Mother, doors are to be opened. Anyway, how am I supposed to take care of them? I've got to be able to stick my hand in to change their water, give them their birdseed—she replied, her voice a thundering laugh.

—It's gone—I remember with sadness.

—Well, it's smarter than the one who stayed.

Dying isn't a tragedy to her because she's young. When I tell her: "Leaving is like dying a little," she thinks I'm being pretentious. "Oh, Mother, get with it." She teaches me something, I don't know what, but something. Then in complete defeat I add:

—These birds are defenseless; they're used to someone putting food in their little beaks.

I glance across the garden. I don't want to find it on the ground.

—Where could it have flown to?—I ask, devastated. Then I add glumly: life doesn't make sense.

—Of course it does—my daughter trumpets. It's the only thing that does make sense.

—How?

—It makes sense all by itself.

When it gets dark, I bring the canary that didn't know to escape inside. Against my will, I feel a certain contempt for him; slow, clumsy, he missed his chance. I find a place for the cage.

The next day, I take him out into the light in this new ritual imposed by my daughter. "It's your bird." I try to whistle at him, but I can't. I call him "pretty" as I hang the cage on the nail, suspended slightly in the air so that the prisoner thinks he's flying. I return to my chores, the limp stockings on the chair, yesterday's slip, the book I'll never read, the eyeglasses that are going to get scratched if I don't put them away, God, an unmade bed is so ugly. What did I awake to? Suddenly, I hear a lively chirp, carefree, a few cascading trills, his singing interrupts the morning sluggishness. He warbles, his sharp arpeggios fill the terrace, Conchita Square, what heavenly music his trills, Mozart. Other birds respond to his harmonies. At least that's what I think. It's the first time he has sung since he arrived. Is it for his darker-feathered companion that he fills space with so much laughter? I try not to care. How does something so small and barely yellow manage to cause such a ruckus in a tree? When I was a little girl and would eat pumpkin seeds, my mother would say, "An orange tree is going to grow inside you." Or an apple tree. The idea thrilled me. Now it's the canary that causes a tree to grow inside me. I echo. I'm made of wood. His singing has unleashed something. Mine is a sad house, stuck in time, a house full of monotonous rituals, tidy; he lets loose now; I'm alive, he says to me, look at me, I'm alive.

His singing causes a tiny ship to sail from my branches, the wind that drives it is pure energy, time flows at last, I dive in, I make the bed, open my arms, kneel, tidy up, bend over, go, come, I can't stop now, his singing inspires me to be something else, I go out to the terrace to see if he needs anything, I walk on tiptoes, not wanting to jeopardize this newfound happiness for anything in the world, so much eagerness, I greet him, "handsome, handsome," "thank you, thank you," "handsome, handsome," "thank you, thank you," I laugh to myself, I realize that I haven't laughed in months, silence sings between the walls, I unveil a house that sings, the canary is my heart, he trembles yellow, the light of heaven whistles in his tiny breast.

Translated from the Spanish by George Henson

Exodus

When the time came to leave I looked around
for something to glue me together, see one through, I knew
perfectly well this wasn't fatal, ah but

the interim
between relinquishing keys & getting the next set & for what & from whom —
Ah that:

Being without I mean, defranchised, bereft, chattels in storage & goods up for grabs,
penates & lares in diverse valises not labelled in my chaos which was
one more complication:

At moments like these, seismics, it behooves us
to swivel to the left reducing volumn to nil, switch from Boil
to Simmer & so it was I knelt, at some point, in the midst,

at a box of old patterns marked
Simplicity
of which the most appealing, God knows why, such a goofy mess

of unnecessariousness, who ever learns, was a bunch of some bathrobe-type things,
elastic-bonded: a sorority: what I might have been wrapped in
chilly evenings if I'd ever learned to sew: here were the bare bones:

esoteric kimonos, merengue-ish negligees, garments to sling on
blithe, after the bath, to seduce in or be thus, to fry eggs
on foggy mornings, to kiss goodnight flannelly any number of

offspring I never produced: costumes
for every occasion & none of them used —
knees on the floor that was bare & unaccustomed, head everywhere

I think I thought: talisman. I took them along

Poema para formar un río

Con la saliva que gastaron mis enemigos
para injuriarme
construí un río
en el que navego por las noches
con sus novias o sus hermanas.

Con las piedras que me lanzaron
construí la casa
en la que vivo como un rey.
Si las pedradas siguen
haré un condominio, lo venderé y seré rico
mientras ellos ejercen su derecho
a patalear de envidia.

Con las balas que me tiraron
construí un árbol de pólvora:
al encenderlo se forma la vía láctea.

Con las palabras que me arrojaron
escribí varios libros.
Cuando se dieron cuenta
que en vez de enemigos
eran mis mejores publicistas
exigieron regalías.

Agotado su almacén
de palabras, balas, piedras,
me declararon poeta nacional.

Yo sigo
escribiendo poemas en servilletas,
de chulo por las calles
de una ciudad que ni siquiera es la mía.

Ahora que están muertos
siento que algo me falta.

Poem for Constructing a River

With the saliva spent by my enemies
to wound me
I built a river
in which I sail at night
with their fiancées or sisters.

With the stones they threw at me
I built a house
in which I live like a king.
If they keep stoning me
I'll make a condominium, I'll sell it and be rich
while they exercise their right
to stomp about in envy.

With the bullets they shot at me
I built a tree of gunpowder:
when lit it turns into the Milky Way.

With the words they hurled at me
I wrote several books.
When they realized
that instead of enemies
they were my best publicists
they demanded royalties.

When they finally ran out
of words, bullets, stones
they declared me poet laureate.

I keep on
writing poems on napkins,
like a pimp on the streets
in a city that's not even mine.

Now that they're dead
I feel like I'm missing something.

Translated from the Spanish by Steven J. Stewart

Vida de los animales y las plantas

La luz es importante para la respiración de los peces y la movilidad de las
       esporas.
El sabor de la sandía es rojo.
El sueño de la mar es verde.
Un vaquero juega con una vaca pinta en la sala de su casa.
Una mujer desnuda, a cualquier hora del sueño, es un peligro para el tráfico.
Gonzalo Rojas piensa en Monterrey.
El río suena: la fórmula del vidrio es inversamente proporcional a la vida de
       los peces y al destello de las esporas.
La textura de una mata de pelo aparece en la lente del microscopio como una
       bugambilia imaginada por el sol.
La mixtura de tu piel es necesaria para la respiración de las plantas.
Yo soy una planta.

The Life of Animals and Plants

Light is necessary for the breathing of fish and the movement of
      spores.
Watermelons taste red.
The sea dreams green.
A cowboy plays with a spotted cow in his living room.
A naked woman is a traffic hazard at any hour of the night.
Gonzalo Rojas meditates on Monterrey.
The river speaks: the formula of its glassiness is inversely proportional to the life
      of the fish and the discontinuity of the spores.
The texture of a sprig of hair appears in the lens of a microscope like a
      bougainvillea shrub imagined by the sun.
The composition of your skin is necessary for the breathing of the plants.
I am a plant.

Translated from the Spanish by Steven J. Stewart

Lineage

I

The jasmine tree released its scent
Onto the summer evening. Punctually
I was sent forth. She sat in the twilight
After watering the roses. My bare feet
Sopping the wetness of her patio floor.
I ignored the little chair beside her
And climbed up on her lap. In one hand
She held the beads of her rosary,
With the other she caressed my braids.
Like the breath of a single creature
We would pray, my grandmother whispering
Her half of the Hail Mary and I proudly
Reciting the rest of the chant.

One Sunday morning, after Mass, a boy
And I giggled on that same patio floor.
From the window she saw as he suddenly
Kissed me. I was fourteen years old.
Mare came out of the house with her hands
On her hips, her lips trembling. Behind her
The angry angel with the flaming sword.
She stood on the sidewalk of our street
For a long time looking at oncoming traffic.
Love evaporating like summer rain.
Outrage building a road that led to this:
"I want your name omitted from my obituary,
I don't want people to wonder how you live."

II

Spinster Aunt Francisca formed with Mare
The perennial pair. With heads of gray hair
They marched arm in arm through the store
Unsoundly. With lips pursed, noses wrinkled
Looking with disdain at the vegetables.

Mistrusting the checker, double-checking
The butcher. At the kitchen table Fanny
Fixed iced coffee while everyone napped.
Offered me dishes born out of idleness:
Artichokes with marshmallows, mustard
On coffeecake. All the maids
Were accused of laziness. Timo,
Timotea, the only one patient enough to stay.

In the afternoons Fanny would drive
The children to dance lessons, if we gave her
Enough time to find her keys. When it rained
We had to cancel; she wouldn't move
Her "precious cargo" if the pavement was wet.
She would take us out to dinner and pack
In embroidered linen her own silverware.
Since I was a "fallen woman" Fanny felt free
To say vulgar, embarrassing things
To me. I would nod with the detachment
Of the anthropologist. Only her view about
Money has consequences: "Poverty," she said
"Will be more fitting to your bohemian life."

III

My mother did not fuss. She embarked upon
Her day like a treasure hunt. She allowed for
Seconds spent at traffic lights, counting on
Shortcuts she would find. I waited
Knowing my tasks would be listed and
Explained only one time. Before lunch, Mami
Revealed to friends our finds: "The tablecloth
To match your set is at Dehner's main floor.
Watermelons are ripe and dahlias gold
At the stand on Second Avenue." If she fixed dinner
She would open the refrigerator just twice.
If she misplaced a receipt for the cleaners
She would simply post a monetary reward.

When I could not sleep at night, I'd sit outside
Her bedroom door.   Her whimpering entwined
With father's roaring snore. He prescribed her
Valium and vitamins, it didn't always work.
The news of cancer in her brain was God's
Invitation to a celestial event, which
She longed to attend. Towards the end,
In the hospital pharmacy she found
A card, scribbled my name and placed
A crooked stamp. Inside, set against
Our silence, a Hallmark rhyme.
She underlined the words: "my lovely child"
And managed to sign. Your mother, Trinidad.

Sam Joyner, photograph

A story red with dawn

I know a story you must know.
I will tell it as I learned it
but if you listen
you can hear them
telling in the blackberry
around the taco truck
at the crook-legged table
of a one-room apartment
they are telling a story.
It is a story that we
need to hear.

i.

In San Martin Peras
I recognize seven-thirty a.m.
by the way the sun slivers
through the thatched roof.
Popocatepetl sits not as volcano
but as shadow on dawn's horizon
a faraway mountain haloed with ash
cradled by the cornfield's whisper.
Children lead me these mornings
on their walk to school as Josefina
drills me on my daily lesson
tskiva means butterfly
tchina means dog
ita means flower
inshishi'ni for hair *
In the yard boys in government-issued
navy-blue sweatshirts call out *Gusikye!*
inviting me to basketball while girls
collect fistfuls of pollywogs to give me.
After school I visit Reyna who shifts
baby Fidel from one breast to the other

*From the Mixtec, one of the indigenous languages of
Mexico.

as I help her decipher picture books
ca-sa   ga-to   ga-llo
For dinner the family shares a can of beans
and yellow ears from behind the house
that Cecilia turns on the fire.
On the day fever keeps me
in bed past noon Marcelina
brings me warm tea in a *jícara*
as Florencio twines his fingers in my hair
making a waterfall of my spine.
Emilio and Celestino guide me
by both my hands when I head
down a trail-less slope
to where guavas grow lonely
by the river.
                    Nana lifts tortillas
from her *comal* when we return
and the sweet sweetness of
chilacayote squash fills our bellies.
Then November with her fiestas arrives.
Rutilia hikes me up to the *panteón*
to show me the headstones flowering
with candles copal marigold arcs
children playing tag between ice cream carts
grandmothers grandfathers singing *Ave María*
in their Mixtec ancestors' tongue.
These nights the town spills
into its plaza turned dance hall
where the band plays
chilenas until two a.m.
and after midnight
when entrance is free
all of San Martin Peras sways
and skips along.
After the last *atole* sells
and light bulbs short out
we huddle four to a mattress
between adobe walls.
Breath nearing silence

eyelids drawn over her dreams
Cecilia blankets me with arms.
We sleep.

ii.

After six weeks I
zip shut my bag
hop into the back of a rusty pickup
pay the driver twenty pesos to
take me down the dirt road
sixty pesos to Huajuapan then seventy
to Mexico City where I board a
two-hundred-dollar flight to L.A.

Back in California
I dread mornings.
They push past me
like cars cramped
on a rush-hour freeway
coughing along cement carpets
smothering the landscape.

I need to return
to hear little Irma run to me pleading
Swing me around! Ka ve! Ka ve!
to reach for her hands and spin
faster and faster until red adobe homes
and gray mountains stretch into
a blurred rainbow and I can no longer see
where this town ends and my life beyond begins

iii.

Two years later I do return
to see how things change and discover
how sadness hovers old and deathless
as the church. The skeleton child
who grunted after bread crumbs
on the yellow steps of the municipal building

has vanished. The dirt road
that once coiled up from below
the river and stretched like a tongue
through the center of town
now lies stiff with cement
a little more dignified a little less
familiar along the plaza.
Don Aldino is still here. He and his wife
have stayed in their green snack stand selling
instant noodles to visiting doctors
and cloud-pink candy to children. Doña Tere
like an iron pot fills the same space
behind her stove. Magdalena now eighteen
stirs beans beside her mother and still
has not seen the river. Baby Gerardo
died. Reyna tells me this but did not count
the months since his stomach swelled
and they carried him to the *panteón*.
Fidel walks now and talks and asks
who I am. There is a new baby too
wearing red ribbons in her ponytails
and a smudge-faced doll on her back in a sling.

The morning I arrive Rutilia plants tears in my lap
and in my palms the photos she weeps over every day.
They are snapshots of us before the pavement
and the baby, before her cousins left North.
The sadness clings to Rutilia like a communion dress
a white lace blouse, straight white skirt
jacket stretched over her chest
by a fake gold chain. This is how
she wears it in the picture.

Rutilia takes me to meet her sister
but we cannot converse. I speak
English and Spanish. Her sister
speaks the language from the land.
Her sister sits thin against the house
she shares with dangling meat
and a husband who lives mostly

in California. She offers me dried beef
an apple from her tree and words
for Rutilia to interpret.
She is happy to see you, Rutilia reports
She says she will miss you when you leave.
These people have gone North—
Rutilia's older brothers, years gone.
Florencio who at eight years old
sold chiclets on the streets of Nuevo Leon
and at seventeen walked me to the edge
of the *panteón* and in the misty hills of his birth
could pick out only sadness.
Florencio went back North. His new wife
and baby went too and did not come home
for the fiestas this year. Celestino also left
crossed for the first time with his cousin Emilio
who sent a photo of himself sitting on a brick
fireplace in a Salinas living room. Reyna tells me
the camera makes his dimples too deep
her husband's face surprisingly full.
Rutilia and Lucia now plan to leave, too.

This is who returned:
Marcelina's husband
after three silent years.

I have also returned, a visitor
bearing these gifts from my journey
an embroidered napkin,
rebozos from Juxtlahuaca,
my favorite red sweatshirt
which Cecilia pulls over her purple dress.
It is an offering from the other side.

I live on the other side
el otro lado where I was born.
I have plastic cards and stamped papers
to prove it. I purchase my corn
for a quarter an ear. The people I know
die of cancer and age. I have never

seen a toddler's belly swell on the other side.
On the other side, I read
the newspapers. This is how I know
that a Mixteca in Fresno is missing
an eye and that her eye was swallowed
by poison from the field. I know
that a Peras family was interviewed
in Santa Cruz, and a Mixteco in Oxnard
voted pro-union. I know
he picks strawberries there.

I know that on a day-trip to Tijuana
I could turn the corner and name
the child who waves a styrofoam cup
at my chest and that child
may remember my face and I
might ask (though I already know)
What are you doing so far from home?
I know the supermarket sells
Watsonville strawberries
that Florencio's fingers
may have picked
because I have seen
the photo of Florencio
posing beside a truck
in a field of vines
his right foot
on a crate of red fruit
as if to conquer the harvest
before the load rolls away.
I know the first three days after leaving San Martin
passengers on the contractor's bus have only
stale tortillas to eat. I know the border fence
shoots further east every year. I know
the desert walk is endless.
I know no one sleeps well
on a cardboard mattress
in the fields.

And I know *chilenas*
songs with beats that trot
like the fiesta's children
melodies that wind like
mountains trails around the heart.
These songs born in Chile
traveled North to nest in Oaxaca
and continue North in the duffle bags
of migrants. Florencio owns *chilenas*
on cassette. It's the only thing he takes
North with him to remind him of home,
the only thing at home he will dance to.

I don't know what Peras sounds like
after the fiestas when only elders
and toddlers and some mothers stay.
I don't know what it is to arrive
on the other side without cash
and with only a language
nobody will hear. I don't know
what it means for Reyna to sleep
alone with little growing Fidel.
I don't know what it means that
no one has seen Rutilia's brothers
in Tijuana or in Oxnard or in Salinas
where the town regroups among interminable rows.
I don't know what the photos mean to Rutilia.
I don't know why Gerardo is dead.
I don't know what one red sweatshirt
a blue *rebozo*
fifty pesos
five dollars
means to the family
who has none.

There is sadness here, Florencio said.
As he spoke it slid like a lifeless bird
down the angles of his cheeks.
Florencio said,
Hay mucha tristeza aquí.

iv.

Listen
this season and for every season more
strawberries bleeding in my blender
will look like a horizon
red with ash and dawn and
adobe-speckled hills.
I will hear not the motor
but the one-legged rhythm of *chilenas*
and I will know what I know
that somewhere in a city I drive through often
they are telling a story.

It is a story we need to hear.

James H. Young, *Maria*, photograph

When I Clap

My right hand reaches for the feather of memory
that fell from my mother's hat as she bent to get out
of the car, down tugged away on wind, not unlike
the pigeon, roosting now above the church door, satisfied
with alcove. Everything I touch is the texture of oven bread,
round like my mother's voice as I teach her conversation again.
The scent of *empañadas* lingers in the blue opal earthstone
of her earring when she leans to say *Goodnight, God bless,
until morning,* but now, I say the words first because she
has forgotten even the sound firetrucks make outside our window.
What's that? she asks, her palms pressed to her ears.

My left hand smells of the street dog I just stroked
and fed a scrap of bread. His eyes follow me, food to mouth.
He is only the dog smell clinging to my sleeve. His cold nose
pokes my hand, my bare knee, my crotch. When I open my palm
to strike him, he turns to me, the one he will not bite, the one
he will smell again and again. I've never touched that cloud
outside the plane window, though I've wanted to ever since
I was a child and looked up to the dinosaur, the whale, a giant face,
all vapor, all change, all the promise of rain above my head.

I've lost the questions. Each word like a hundred shards
scuttles across the floor. It is not like the cup, glass, china plate.
It makes no sound, but a flavor hovers from the wreckage: onion,
garlic, cinnamon, *cebolla* with a scent of burning underbrush.
When I reach for the apron, tie the knot behind my back,
memories fall into the braided hair of my daughter. My palms
knead bread, shape loaves, set trays in ovens. My nails
are softened by white flour that clings, leaves fingerprints
on everything I touch. When I bring my hands together they are
not the *empañada.* They are not folded with the blend of *atún,
cebolla, pimiento.* They are not hands that seal at the edges.
They are not hands that stay together. They are not hands.

I've touched the answer, but unlike the dog, it left. Even answers
chase pigeons until they lift towards the church alcove. You can't hear

flapping wings until the bird is above you, and these pigeons think
I have bread. They gather. They coo. They fly startled when I celebrate
my open palms in their direction. It is not the sound of snow. It is not
the sound of rain. It is not weather. It is a broom lapping cool stones.
It is my mother cleaning the patio.

Francisco Toledo, drypoint

Kafkaesque No. 1 (Nogales)

For Barry Shapiro

After too many drinks I drink the water and soon
I'm wandering the desert expecting it to tell me
what I need to know. You're there, Shap, bug-

eyed like K., and right at home among the anchorites
and saguaros and the billion ants that sound like
a trillion castanets; later we metamorphose into

the moles of our college days and the moles become
beetles and the beetles professorial dogs and the dogs
apes screeching for their fathers' hearts and the apes

wrens with hollow bones and the wrens Heraclitus
who reminds himself (us) that it all comes down to παντα ρει,
i.e., nothing can live without changing into something else;

while *self-satisfaction, because it's static, will always be punished*.
Then the ants click, the anchorites moan and the saguaros
wave their handless arms and, without warning, bloom.

Puerto

La ciudad sabe a mar,
da campanazos de salitre,
mece los brazos largos de sus sauces,
lame los ateridos huesos de sus plátanos,
se escapa en una enmarañada deserción.
Mueve los pies frenética en el cielo,
baila en el viento y en el agua,
y zapatea sus choclos con la lluvia, tap, tap.
Corre desesperada de callejón en callejón,
huye como si fuera la misma niebia,
y se va a pique con todo su ruidero.
Y más abajo el alma humana, su humareda, su chimenea,
su montón de infiernillos y discordias,
sus mil pasos prendidos a cada día.
Un inmenso mar de luciérnagas,
el puerto,
sus hombres y mujeres.

Harbor

The city tastes like the sea,
tolls bells of salt residue,
sways the long arms of willows,
laps the cold core of plantain trees,
escapes into tangled abandon.
It moves its frenetic feet in sky,
dances in wind and in water,
and clicks its heavy clogs with rain, tap, tap.
It runs desperate from alley to alley,
flees as if it were the fog itself,
and capsizes with all its noisemakers.
And beneath its human pulse, its cumulus, its chimney,
its heap of little hells and discordance,
its thousand steps ignite each day.
An immense sea of fireflies,
the harbor,
its men and women.

Translated from the Spanish by Katie Kingston

Tizonal

Los actos de la vida se juntan en palabras,
chocan en sus sentidos, se patean,
huyen pulverizados y obstruidos,
como un alambre que se quiebra en su furia
en la erizada violación del viento.
En el ahogo de la garganta se enciende el aire.
Fuera,
desamparadas cañas,
desolados escombros en el campo pizcado,
trizados y quebrados despojos de la mañana,
en el abandono en el que quedan
a la llegada de las secas:
un varerío
por el que mascan y triscan toros y vacas,
un varerío que hay que quemar también
para que la tierra se caliente.

Charred Acreage

The acts of life come together in words,
they collide in meaning, kick,
flee pulverized and obstructed,
like a wire that crackles in rage
in the prickly violation of wind.
In the anguish of the throat the air ignites.
Outside,
deserted reeds,
desolate debris in the harvested field,
fragmented and broken plunder of the morning,
the abandon of what is left
upon the arrival of dryness:
brambles
where bulls and cows chew and trample,
brambles that need to burn too
in order to warm the earth.

Translated from Spanish by Katie Kingston

The Written Word

After reading Rilke's text
entitled "Urgeräusch"

Where might I have written the lines
which now make up this poem?
At what juncture of time and space
—conundrum of experiences made up—
wrote I what seems that I say here?
Because I'm sure that in the marrow
of these sounding and spelled bones
it has been written by someone like myself
—if not by me—
who thinks my name is such and so
and who is called just as I call myself.
And what if this had only been thought up?
That does not matter.
To think is to write as it is written
in the frontal suture of the skull,
perhaps also in the creases of the brain
like folds of paper
wet with salt from ancient tree-like seas
such as the corals living in their depths.
To speculate is to reflect what has been written
in those grooves reached barely by the wind,
erasing everything it can erase, even what seems
to be more indelible than silence.
That reflection is then thought and later written
in gray ink by ideas resembling tentacles
which are the insubstantiality of our feelings.

Everything is written except what can't be written.
And yet what has been written is suddenly erased
by currents of rivers, transparent like glass,
ageless nurture turned into fisher's nets.
What I have written here, if I have written right,
will also not remain.
Fishing is artful

and barely a magic trick using hands and sleeves.
From every line remains hardly a thing
of what at one time swam, of what at one time passed
in the waters of some consciousness.

But then I don't recall
what I believe I either phrased or paraphrased.
Could it be that the needle of the mental phonograph
stopped plowing the furrows of the brain,
preventing all ability to write
and making all wise and eager words
lose their veracity?

Los viajeros

toda coincidencia es una cita
desordenada música en la mano
de un ángel que cierra los ojos
al otro lado puede ser del mundo
a donde estás a punto de partir

qué hilo en las fibras
del papel que sale de tus manos
secretamente nos reúne o nos inventa
esta tarde esta lluvia de julio pensarías
quién soy qué recuerdo cuál inocultable rostro
de los que tu imaginación ha convocado cuál
entre esta gente reunida por el agua
será quien ya te recuerda
mientras llueve
al otro lado del mundo

porque cada coincidencia es también esa cita
que hicimos en el sueño
y al despertar olvidamos
un instante tal vez otro camino fijado
en el reverso transparente de tus pasos
y ese lugar al que volvemos
creyendo que nos vamos

Travelers

every coincidence is an appointment
out-of-tune music in the palm of the hand
of an angel who is closing her eyes
on the other side as it were of the planet
where you are just about to travel

what thread in the fibers
of the paper just dropping from your hands
secretly brings us together or invents us
this afternoon this rainy july you might think
who am i what memory what unconcealable face
out of all those your imagination evoked who
among all these people rejoined by water
will be the one who still remembers you
when it's raining
on the other side of the planet

because every coincidence is also that appointment
which we made in a dream
and forgot upon waking
an instant maybe another path defined
by the reversed transparency of your footsteps
and that place to which we return
in the belief that we are leaving

Translated from the Spanish by John Oliver Simon

issa

porque nos vamos borrando
de la superficie tensa del agua
y lo sabemos

hemos estado allí tan escrupulosa tan severamente
el mundo nos dibujó
que lo creímos
creímos estar para siempre
en esa fiesta delgada de la luz

pero no hay ofensa ni defecto

estuvimos allí

en la dicha y el duelo invitados por una razón
que no supimos

alevosía

será entonces la belleza que nos hace mirar una vez (con eso basta) su
        rostro

que para siempre se irá trazando

que para siempre se irá borrando

Issa

because we are being erased
from the surface of water
and we know it

we've been there the world sketched us
so severely so scrupulously
that we believed it
we believed we would remain forever
in this slender festival of light

but there's no offense nor blame

we were there

in happiness and in sorrow invited for some reason
we never found out

betrayal

so it would be beauty which made us see (once
        is enough) her face

which is being sketched forever

which is being erased forever

Translated from Spanish by John Oliver Simon

Kill-Box

1.

The air at first smells only of cool steel and chaff.

The air isn't fresh but isn't so old—at a standstill, let's say, a halt
on a spur track there in the train-yard.

The air—and by the air
I mean the cube of breathable space inside the boxcar—

isn't going to be enough.

Meaning the total number of available breaths.
Human breaths.

Which you could tally out, divided by the number of stowaways on board,
to figure how much time the 11 of them—

even as the train was picking up speed out of Matamoros, however long ago,
mid-day, mid-way into June, snaking its way across the border—

have left. Which (again) isn't enough.

They're inside the grain hopper, the 55 foot long 15 high 100 ton Union
        Pacific boxcar
with 3 compartments and center loading hatch.

Our passengers aren't anybody to speak of.
They're not newsworthy yet.

What matters about them, the 11 of them, why they're even in there,
is their illegality—

which on this particular day, under this sun,

having just come to a stop, somewhere in Oklahoma, evening now,
having failed to make their connection, and no one in earshot,

is, at least for them, what keeps all their attention on breathing.

Isn't it getting trickier to keep track of things—air, sense, syntax, the line, etc., someone thinks from inside wherever.

Isn't it starting to get a bit hot in here, another thinks from a corner of the box.

2.
4 women, 7 men.
Paid a *coyote* $1500 each for the ride.
The hatch locked from outside.

This according to the sources who afterward sort out situations like this—

a border agent, a clerk, reporters on deadline, all of whom file such incidents in the cumulative keeping track of these kinds of bodies—

these who got up one morning and went about the ordinary business of smuggling themselves into a boxcar, and crossed.

And that now, among themselves, begin to murmur yes,

yes it does seem to be getting hot.

———————————

The garden at my place is an old garden somebody else planted.

I've been taking care of it for a while now,
I whack at it and prune the fringes and stake what falls over
in the mid-summer heat, but, still,

it keeps insisting on going almost wild, and arguing's not much use.

Anyone who knows anything about gardens wouldn't call this
a civilized sort of haven.

Whoever designed it —
ages ago, I'm guessing, by the cast of the shadow of the apple tree —
must've had in mind the making of a sanctuary, a place of rest.

I can imagine the gardener studying the microclimate,
taking notes on the global-positioning of the light at set times of day

in order to custom-plant the border that runs the length of the yard.

Still, so many invasives
sprout every spring like mad and run rampant through what's planted.

Ribbon-grass sprints across the walk.
Stonecrop steals into whatever crevice it wants, and the spring poppy crop
riots like a black-eyed full-blaze wildfire.

3.
It must've been a kind of freedom they figured they were about to
happen into. No matter how it got lost

in translation along the way, in the beginning

it was as if it might occur to them —

getting across, getting free, as if they might almost by chance
encounter it, enter its territory, its state, and, suddenly, in the instant
of demarcation, be ever after able to stay there,

the way any of us giving it enough thought could narrate our own backstories
into a before and an after the fill-in-the-blank event

(the birth, the death, the siren, the call, the lapse, the scouring-out of the mind
through one long night and, then, at the end of it,

the illuminated clearing —).

As if the border were that crease.

As if it might have been a way to alter the itinerary of their fates

that veered off course and into these salt-flats, five hours past a hundred
        degrees,
now that the water's run out,

though right now they're just concerned
with starting to shift, to murmur, to panic and even, a few, freak, and bang,

bang, bang.

As if.

4.
About this garden that's disintegrating.
About this dry teasing heat yesterday's accumulating cumulous clouds
meant to fix.

The last iris slaves on.

About this spiral of dust starting to rise into the air like a startled girl's throat.

And these birds that crane their heads into the drought
that just this morning blew the heads off the purple thistles.

About the wind aiming at the fence it means to break its spine on.
About the fence, that won't relent.

5.
About the plume of dust that had risen in their wake
and now settles.

About the proving ground, about the drift of filings, flecks, of splinters
        and chaff
that litters it and is visible

to no one. About the no one
in earshot.

There is a wall upon the flat salt earth —
something there is about it that isn't going to let them go,

something about its very nature that isn't going to give us knowledge
of just what it was took place in the souring air it traps.

How long did the banging on it go on?

Exactly what sort of noise did the collateral spray of their one last bang
          on this hot
communicating wall make?

That no one heard as it rippled out?
Metallic, the odor of a bloodied fist, into the lot — anyone?

Haven't we asked these questions of boxcars before?

6.
Right about now the evening sky's ripe
for a mid-season shower of fire off falling stars, flowering fires late in the
          far-off fields

according to the forecast, which follows the breaking
news that we're living now in a "target-rich environment,"

as it's put by those whose say-so seems to describe the current state of
precariousness as a prediction,

a weather just now coming into being on its way here, and worsening,

in this lot ringed by hallowed, fallow wilderness that answers
the passing of trains in the dusk

merely by trembling.

———————————

The gilded larches deliver their knock-down argument in favor of the
         reckoning
summer-singed light

even as the garden's busy being beautiful
burning.

There's nothing but sinkholes left of the thousand and then some ephemerals
         that
blew open under the dead leaves, and soon fled at the threat of heat.

Now the garden's stunned, sunstruck at dusk.

Against the bruised skyline lean the hurt stalks.
Rioting aphids overrun the patch of phlox no one's tended in weeks.

There's so much pollen in the air by now it's as if a sepia coats the day,
and the daylilies release their daylong blooms like a sigh let out of the ground.

Turns out most of what goes wrong in a garden

does without meaning to,
without malice, without fault, without meaning.

7.
As soon as the sun goes down, they swarm.
As soon as the map goes black, they come running crawling fleeing.
Come at the border in a drill across the hardpan at it and at it.

The noise of buzzing goes with it.
It's this buzzing the traffic of their bodies kicks up that won't quit.

It works into the inner ear, it sticks and won't, on anyone in earshot, have
         mercy
and quit.

The grit holds the day's heat.

According to their feet the border's a predicament—
this stampede across it, this flushing out into the dark run of the flatland,

this rushing fast of five, six hundred bodies a night out of the makeshift shanty
       camps

the wind's gusted up against, this dune of ash blown into a bias
as the exodus starts at dusk, all their gazes trained on the sky,

fastened there on the firmament waiting for the light to die.

Around Naco, stadium floods switch on and hit the terrain with hot white
       fluorescence
the locals call house lights.

Into it *coyotes* send decoys at just past twilight, the opening salvo.

Then the wave hits, quailing in panic over open ground.

Every night it's this script and the next and every next night and whoever's
       snagged
goes at it all over again the next after that.

In Matamoros, they race at the dark cars and scale up and wedge in and wait
       for the click
of the latch.

In Tijuana they cram behind dashboards and cross the checkpoints with bruises
the shapes of springs and jacks and knobs blooming in their skins.

In Calexico they float on hitched logs in a reeking green stream that's skinned
       in trash.

In Nogales there's a tunnel that runs a quarter-mile—when a crosser inside
       faints
whoever's next crawls in and yanks them back by the ankles and then goes.

One field report calls the stopping of these incursions a basic exercise
in swatting flies.

8.
I come into the garden to kill rampant dill-weed at dusk.
The light says what's been unleashed this season can't be stopped

and whatever might have been on fire still is—sunflowers, asters,
in the downslide of these bat-roiled late twilit hours

when the mind with its static of thought thrums in its want of some rest.

In the stadium across the freeway there's a game on—the players, just kids,
and their fans and a band going at it for all they're worth.

Over here, on this side, each green stalk that's been seized by the day's
        blazing
hazards the unfurling of its head into the dimming light

that at this time of day seems always at risk
of slipping free of all government and going off into free air.

Pine green, olive green, emerald green, tea green, forest green, sage green,
        ultra green,
clover green, electric green, panic green

with the ecstatic vibrato of crickets like an undertow,
and then the feel of ok, yes, something approaching a calm.

Then the thought that feeling just about anything—grief, bliss, distress, you
        name it—
might by now feel like enough.

Then the wanting to be able to come to a rest here and the actual being
        able to
even farther apart than ever,

with the eschatology of every twilight this sense of being scoured out in
        the trying.

On the other side of the traffic,
one team scores and triggers wild cheering, a cannon fires, a fight song
        starts up and
plays itself out

in mid-air, scattering the assembled swallows like scraps of ash across the sky.

The relentless, restless season stumbles across this garden.

The brittle nesting stains green against the acrid soil while this constant
       wakefulness
wears away the bedding's sheen, and orderliness sunders.

One reason for bothering at all is fireflies,
which defibrillate the wrecked shrubs and rise from the understory
like turbo-candles, in flames.

Another is the wall that's burning,
as if there are rules in play now, here, in the garden, we've never imagined.

What's taken over our place is this fine grit, this pittance of law upon the
       scorched leaves,
as the dusk-to-dawn floodlights stutter on, spurred by hollow chiming
through the sore weed-stalks

—and then the cheering begins again in the stadium across the way
as fans set off a human wave.

9.
Later, we get talking about how all our talking about all this could go forever.
Meanwhile, fall's set in

and a train starts up along a track in Oklahoma, and the boxcar in question
picks up speed along with it, in succession,

and comes to a stop finally in Denison, Iowa, in the switching yard there,
in the smallest of blind spots.

It's flatland, it's October, the grain's milled already, it's gone through and used,
what this landscape's good for is already done for and now it's at rest.

Along the tracks, some rough weed—dashing grasses, the goldenrod
that so freely self-seeds.

This is the quiet perilousness that occurs in October, in the air

when it's blown across the fields and into town,
which I know from coming from around here.

What's in the works is a harsh winter again,
you can tell by the way the cut shocks buckle and crack after the hard
       freeze hits,
and then kneel down in the killing frost.

It's not going to go again
with them in it.

It's not clean. It's not dry or ready or empty, it's just not,

when, on a Sunday, in this late autumn, a worker at the Farm Service
       Co-op elevator
pries open the sealed hopper brought in after a summer in a storage lot
       out west
and happens on the remains.

The banging of course has stopped.

Way back there, in June.

As the last alternative outcome molted off, and fate turned into
a dizzying, spectacular wind

that's even now, even here, causing the birds to whirl up like soot from
       these trees.

10.
A bitten crust.
Fist prints on the wall. Ash. A shoe.

I come out as the storm starts its blowback operation upon the garden.

Whatever bloomed is shut again, and the wind's climbed
from the hollows to shear whatever's too high for its liking.

The late-blooming hazels are past ripe though the odor they give off seems
almost
to keep these hours afloat,

while our light goes about losing the use of its mind
or is it using the loose of our minds

as the air bears such likeness, in this fall wind, to being skinned.

Can't say what's causing what's growing here to list into the squall
just to stand straight

if not sheer will, even as the wind cranks up

and plays what's left of the maple trunk in minor keys turned off-tune
by drought and core rot

years ago someone opened up by punching a fist through the bark,
so that in going about its cadence —

which is all motion and air — all breath — the gusting

snags on the knots and ring-swells enough to cause a sort of haunted
canting to rise from the ruined wood.

This is a tree that should've given in, in surrender,
to its own systematic imperfection.

It should've been removed from the premises ages ago.

In this garden what's needed to take a thing like this down
isn't weather.

This isn't that kind of garden.

Landscape with Snakes

Our quick-running silver was already
seeping, unseen, back into the slow ground,
closing commerce with the outside, the year
our mother sailed inland on a lotus,
limbs entwined, while her boys went on living
in the long dream of the fathers' fathers
where it was always summer, so it was
late August when we slipped from our cots
beneath the netting of the sleeping porch,
lying under Sanhedrin's shadow, and
swung our rifles up on our shoulders, our
flashlights bobbing in the dark, and parted
the fields of waist-high cheat grass with our thighs
to the edge of the airstrip, where buzzing
like Cessnas above the world, we descended
on brush squats and nests of the cottontails.
Flashing our lights, we spun quick fire into
the soft white fur, and in the spread of blood
became entangled in the fescue grass
of fields our dreamy fathers named Eden.
Rattlers slithered over granite like streaks
of mottled gray light from another world—
we took them for the water of a spring
until heads and tails rose up, framing them—
the wide, wedge-shaped mouths, jointed
rattles dancing like rice-paper, *ts-ka ts,*
ts-ka, as we circled now, fluttery as moths,
while in the summer palace of Sanhedrin,
our mother slept on, coiled in her bed,
and the cold-blooded, at home in Eden,
lay in wait for us, there, among the grasses.

Two Crops

Along with the tar weed
sticking to the ox's rump,
the Branscombes traveled
north toward the Lost Coast
from the Mayacamas.

They took hold in the land,
its folds and creases
rumpled as a man's shirt
laundered in rain water
and dried in the sun.

They stayed a hundred years.
With the grass that traveled
with them taking root
in the fields, their kids fed
the goats, bedded the hens.

This spring, the one crop
reseeded once more in
the good Branscombe soil.
The other's plowed deep
under the graveyard
weeded now by goats

gone wild, under the oaks
where four hens are brooding.

Coyotes

Who'll join me in this room
as the winter séance
starts, wind rattling the pots?
My girls, bending their heads
over their murmuring dolls?
The Sinkyone, whose bones,
deep under the floorboards,
shift and turn in the dark?
The gingerbread men I
shape, as my mind drifts off?
Who now living or dead?
I've been content these years,
my household a refuge,
secure from solitude;
I still hold the world off;
not so much as peering out
after a passing truck,
engine coughing to life
beneath rolls of thunder.
Today I'm restless.
My son bangs the door
on his way to the barn.
I follow his blurred form
through the rain-streaked glass,
soon lose him; I lose
the thread of the girls' talk.
I find myself, instead,
thinking of the coyotes
in the hills, their calls beating
the grass, as I thump the dough,
but they have hunkered down
as we have until spring.
The rain's firing like BBs,
and this rain-soaked boy,
my John, has returned with
a brace of rabbits tossed
on his narrow shoulder.

Los trabajos de la ballena / Whaling Chores

to Onelio Jorge Cardoso

This harbor town you're looking at—with its concrete wharf, its road leading from one end of the village to the other, its brick houses on land's edge where the fishermen live, and its wooden shacks right on the beach where the out-of-towners can get a bite to eat—well, it's a decent town now. But when we first came here, there was nothing but lots of sea and solitude.

I was just a kid back then. And yet, I already knew how to dive down into the oyster and clam beds; when there aren't enough hands, even the little finger can help scare up some food. And that's how it was in the other town. You see, we were few, actually just one family, and there were only three houses in town: my blessed grandfather's, my blessed uncle's, and mother's, though she didn't end up so blessed, since she gambled it all on a sailor who one day came here, stark naked, piloting a boat that had capsized.

❊ ❊ ❊

By the time the rooster started to crow, we'd be up and about, everyone in the three houses heading towards the shore. At that time of day, the sea's like a calm eye that knows nothing about heroics. And from that moment until the fireflies started flashing on and off, the second the sun went down, there was nothing for us to do but struggle against the sea and try to snatch food from its claws.

My grandpa, God bless him, was the best fisherman. You had only to watch him walking down the beach to know he was a sailor, the good old-fashioned kind.

When I'd reach the seashore, Grandpa would already be there, launching the canoe that he himself had dug out from a single treetrunk using hot irons. That's how it was then—a hand-to-hand combat with the sea at all hours—not like it is now, with these motorboats farting their way through the waves.

Grandpa would walk along squashing the foam left by the tide and whistling "The ship's gonna sail away . . ." He'd cross himself with water from the first breaker and then launch his dugout out to sea. Leaping aboard, off he would go, rowing and whistling, right to the edge of the horizon. And there he'd toil away, till the sea boiled in the afternoon sun, which turned the water as red as the scales of a snapper. And then he'd return, whistling, or singing his favorite tune:

> When my pretty Lola on the shore goes
> Dragging a tail which in the evening glows
> The sailors go crazy, their minds astray
> And the ship's navigator loses his way.

He'd beach his dugout in the sand to unload the marvelous catch he had speared, for you see, my grandpa fished only with a harpoon. God knows what thoughts he had at sea, in his solitude, but his harpoon was always ready to stab anything that had scales, a smooth skin, or a shell. And as he landed, we children and grandchildren would rush to help him unload the catch and bring it right to the pots and kettles already set for the big feast. In the meantime, the old man spun yarns about the dangers of the sea and about whales, the biggest sea creatures of all: years ago he had seen schools of them frolicking near the boats since their route passed just a mile off the coast from here. But we had never seen a whale, so we didn't believe a single word he said.

Then one morning, as usual, Grandpa blessed himself with seawater and made his way towards the edge of the horizon. There he fished, staring at the sea without blinking, when all of a sudden he saw an enormous shadow hovering at arm's length below the boat. Fear seeped into his bones until his very skeleton crackled. He prayed for St. Barbara's help, then flung his harpoon at the shadow with every ounce of strength he had left. He closed his eyes, threw himself face down in the boat, expecting death to send him on a journey where he'd be forced to row until he reached purgatory.

But nothing happened. And as nothing happened, Grandpa opened his blessed eye and saw that the sun and the sea were one; emboldened, he opened the other eye and sat up in the boat.

His left hand tightly held the boat's portside while the right held the starboard. He leaned over and saw an enormous shadow with a harpoon embedded in the side and only a tear of blood, moving as if learning to swim in water for the first time.

Grandpa very carefully began pulling in the line and, at each tug, the shadow rose higher. When it broke the surface, the mirror in the old man's eyes shattered; with tears in his eyes, he touched the huge soapy back where the harpoon was buried.

"Holy Moses," he exclaimed, astonished. "It's a whale."

He passed his hand back and forth over the wound and realized that the creature had long been dead, in payment for God knows what crazy adventure.

Grandpa caught the whale on a Tuesday afternoon. He rowed all that night, all the next day, and early Thursday morning we caught a glimpse of him far off in the distance. All along we had feared he'd been swallowed up by the sea. The minute we saw him, we swam out toward the boat as fast as we could.

"What do you have there, Grandpa?" we asked.

"A whale," he announced.

Once ashore, Grandpa directed the whole show. He ordered my uncle to bring him all the harpoons in the three-house village. Then he himself drove them into the whale and instructed us as to how to reel the whale onto the beach.

Everyone in the village pulled the hooklines in till late afternoon on that glorious Thursday. When the moon appeared, that huge creature was already embedded in the sand like a ship run aground. Thousands of fireflies came out that night — I don't know from where — but they all flew over the whale, filling it with lights, making it resemble a huge ship floating in the night. No one slept. We all wanted to clamber up the whale's back. And when my uncle finally made it to the top, the only words out of his mouth were: "It's true, it's a whale."

At daybreak we began carving it up. All the villagers helped to cut, salt, and then dry the filets in the sun. The kettles were set to boil the whale blubber for the oil. We worked all day Friday and Saturday, till we had 53 beer barrels of oil. By Sunday noon flies had taken over the remains of the whale: we could hear only a constant buzzing while we worked. Bands of pelicans and gannets flew over our heads. Seagulls cawed and cawed, not taking their eyes off the whale for a second. By then the trees and rocks in the village were covered with buzzards impatiently spreading their wings in the sun. The dogs, nearly crazy from so much eating and dashing about, howled and barked as they tried to frighten off the birds.

At four in the afternoon, Grandpa said: "The whale's starting to stink."

And we had managed to carve up only half the creature.

By daybreak on Monday, the stench was unbearable. None of us could approach the carcass, which had now been taken over by birds. The dogs, tired of their running and barking, now lounged in the sand. The smell was so strong that some of us nearly fainted; we all ended up locking ourselves inside the three houses. Flies were everywhere, flying even into our eyes and ears. No matter where we went we heard the ground crunching, as we stepped on a tide of ants that came from God knows where, some crawling towards the whale while others retreated, hefting chunks of it.

Grandpa ordered us to wrap handkerchiefs dipped in vinegar around our noses and mouths before leading us on one final assault to free us from the stench. With one hand he fought off the defiant birds, while he threw all the harpoons into the whale's tail. Then we all tried pulling the carcass back into the sea. The hooks, however, couldn't hold onto that rotting hulk any longer; as we tugged them, they just flew up into the air, making an awful, sucking sound. It's one thing to pull a whale ashore with the help of the waves and another thing to push it back into the water against the tide.

Late in the afternoon, Grandpa made us stop. We hurried home, followed by the cawing of the birds. We made our way through clouds of flies, crunching more ants as we went along. At that very moment my uncle asked Grandpa: "What are we going to do now?"

Grandpa crushed an ant with the big toe of his right foot. He then announced: "If we can't take the whale away from the village, we'll have to take the village away from the whale."

And that's how we ended up rebuilding the village down here in San Simon's cove.

Translated from the Spanish by David Unger

All the Ashleys in the World

She doesn't remember her father—well, how could she since she was only a cluster of cells in her mother's womb at the time? Her mother didn't even know she was pregnant yet, she's told Ashley, she wouldn't figure that out till another couple weeks had passed and her period had not arrived. "Do you think I would have taken that risk if I knew I was carrying you?" This was what her mother said some of the times she told the story. Other times she said, "We risked everything, your Papi and me, to make sure you'd have a better life, you'd be born here, a citizen, safe and free."

Ashley's seventh-grade English teacher, Ms. Bernfeld, recently spent one full class session on the uses of irony as a literary device. Too bad no one will ever write a book about Ashley's family. Irony to spare there. Safe and free, Mami? Ya think?

Her father didn't have a better life here. No life at all. He made it across the border, sure, then the turn west across the river, but he didn't last even one full day after that. Their little group of crossers had split up once they waded out of the water, once they walked some more, their clothes drying in the searing heat, spirits cautiously lifting, small smiles to acknowledge that they'd managed the initial hurdles, bottled water to slake their spiking thirst. The land, scattered with sparse bristly sagebrush offering no shade, had held itself flat for a long time, until it started to rise, slightly first then more steeply, a series of uneven undulations warning of the mountainous terrain to come. There was little talk. They saved their breath for the climb, for stepping over cracks in the parched earth, trying not to let piles of pebbles or sudden clumps of tumbleweed trip them up. They walked quickly but carefully, watching for rattlesnakes on the ground, cougars crouched on cliffs. Soon they were wet again, sweat gluing shirts and pants to their chests and butts. Each grateful to have worn a hat, but still they felt the skin on their faces tightening under the desert sun like charred meat on a spit. When they reached the first of the caves—more like cubbyholes, dimples in the ankles of granite giants—they crammed in. They rested briefly, squatting, the roof too low for anyone to stand erect. They breathed the cool clay air layered with the ammoniac stench of bat guano. A few briefly closed their eyes. Then the coyote, whose utterances had thus far been limited to grunts accompanying head nods to point the way, told everyone to listen to what he had to say. Señor Estes, his name was, or at least, Ashley's mother has said, this is what they knew him as. He was older than most of his charges, in his forties probably, deep furrows on his forehead and cheeks, a hard squint, his mien marked by many years skulking through this cracked, craggy wilderness.

He told them they must split up. They had clung close until now. A dozen, together tamping down the terror pumping through each as they tramped onward those first hours, ever farther from home. Now Señor Estes divided them into three. Smaller units, less detectable, and lighter on their feet. If they kept moving in this big cluster the miles ahead would break them, he said. They might every single one be caught and sent back. On the other hand, if they encountered *Migra* agents, or bands of roving drunken vigilantes, which would become more likely the further they progressed, he said, four could scatter and each have a chance of escape, *Gracias a Dios*. They might not all make it but most would.

So they split three ways. The coyote tried to separate Jimena, Ashley's mother, from her husband Rafael. Couples have better success apart, he said, and they could meet up later, in the city. But the newlyweds refused, and so when everyone left the cave, scuttling off in different directions, north-northeast, north-north-west, due north, and Señor Estes back south the way they'd come, Jimena and Rafael were paired with two brothers from Teguci-galpa, teenagers, skinny, sinewy, and as dexterous as squirrels as they maneuvered their way across the rough, jutting landscape. The quartet had memorized their route, repeating after Señor Estes: weave your way among the palos verdes with their yellow flowers, the spiky red ocotillos, and the saguaro, miles upon miles of saguaros, but always forward in the direction I've pointed you, always facing the sun. Move as fast as you can, and stay as low to the ground as possible; the gringos may be scanning with their high-tech instruments from miles away but if you're lucky they'll mistake you for jackrabbits. You'll get thirsty fast, even under those hats your scalp will flame, but save your water for later because later it will be worse. Your cheeks will feel powdery dry like cement and your tongue will crack like a crisp blackened slab of *carne seca*. You will come to a series of strange outcroppings, sharp vertical rock formations unlike any you have seen—some say they resemble a field of ripening corn at the height of the harvest season. By the time you get to them the sky should be darkening. You can slow down a little as you make your way between the basalt husks. You can drink, wet your hair if you'd like. Lie down, two of you at a time, maybe get a half-hour's sleep, if the other two stay alert. A rest will help because next you will have a hard long climb, a sharply ascending ridge, it will take hours, the thorny cactus will tear your clothes if you brush against it, prick your skin, but you'll have to ignore it and climb on. The night gets very cold so, believe me, you'll be glad to keep moving. Finally when you get to the rim you will see below you the city's lights. You should arrive at this point by about midnight, half past at the latest. My partner Señor Contreras will be there to guide you the rest of the way.

It went almost as Señor Estes had said. They would have followed his script perfectly if Rafael hadn't broken his leg halfway to the top. Ashley's mother never knew precisely what tripped him up—and Ashley has always puzzled at how her mother can stand the not knowing—a stone, a narrow nearly invisible rift of the sort that crisscrossed the crisp top crust of earth they trod, some tiny skittering lizard that he swiveled to avoid stepping on. All Jimena knew was that he cried out, his upper torso twisted as his arms windmilled and he toppled, landing hard. Jimena ran to him, and then the two brothers. Fidel and Che their names were, you can't even number how many thousands of brothers are named like that, Ashley's mother has always said. Every time she tells the story of that day she stops at the same place, right here, halfway up the ridge, Rafael has just fallen, his arms cartwheeling, leg bent back, and Fidel and Che, Jimena says, Fidel and Che, so many named like that, and she sighs and she's silent and finally Ashley has to say what about Fidel and Che, Mami, what happened next, which she always regrets because then her mother has to go on and tell. How Rafael yelped, once, twice, and how it echoed, three, four. Four yelps in that open air, and as Fidel, Che, and Jimena ran to him to see what was wrong, to tend to him, as they rinsed out the bloody gash at his knee with the last of their precious water, eyeing the exposed shin bone where it angled out all wrong, bending to help him up, they heard a series of answering shouts from behind them, below, just down the last rise, how close they couldn't tell until suddenly the night brightened—skewers of light flamed skyward, silvery arms racing up to rip down the stars—a series of powerful flares shot from less than half a mile back.

They froze. Chevy and Cuervo logos on tattered t-shirts glinting like black-lit Dayglo posters. A quartet of prey. Paralyzed.

But only for an instant, because then their pursuers shouted again, and Fidel, Che and Jimena hustled the last yards toward Rafael, grabbed him, tugged him upright. The brothers strapped his arms around their necks and recommenced the climb, dragging him between them, Jimena urging them on, *"Andale! Andale!"* in whispers for a moment or two, then suddenly loud, panicky, *"Ay! Los perros!"* For now they heard dogs. Two, three, maybe more, their gravelly barks drawing quickly closer, two yards closer, it seemed, for every yard the hobbled foursome advanced. And then Rafael stopped.

"Andale!" from Jimena again. And from Fidel, *"Andale, muchacho,"* and *"Ay, rápido, por favor"* from Che, but Rafael shook his head and let his arms drop from their shoulders and looked down and told them to go on without him and eased himself to the ground. No, they said, of course we won't go on, don't be crazy, they said, Che kneeling, looking him in the eye and assuring him that together they could make it, Fidel grasping his elbows and trying to force him up. The brothers tussled with Rafael while Jimena pled, whispering a hissing lava flow, don't do this, she begged, you tell me to go ahead but it is you who will be leaving me behind, I can't make it alone, don't abandon me, *mi amor*, we are headed to New York, remember, your cousin Emilio is there, he has room for us, a bed, and he'll help us get jobs, we can make it, Rafaelito, we can make it we can make it. Here, she said, take my hand. He did, but he didn't rise. He pulled her close. He drew her into a kiss. *"Un beso por el momento,"* he said. He kissed her again. *"Y uno más. Para el próximo necesitamos esperar. Pero no llores, Jimena. No tardaré mucho. Volveré pronto. Te lo prometo."* Then he turned. He faced Fidel and Che. He pried their fingers off his elbows and shoulders. He squeezed their hands inside his, pressing against their knuckles with all his force. He rasped a harsh command: "Take her! Go!"

The shouts of their pursuers, closing in. The frenzied caterwauling of the dogs, louder by the minute. Jimena holding onto him, begging, her tears soaking the frayed collar of his t-shirt. The brothers bending. Patting his shoulder, each once, nodding. Taking hold of her. Yanking her up, off him, shushing her, quiet now, we have to go, pulling her, come now, we can't wait anymore, come on, come on, this is what he wants us to do, and he's right, it's the only sensible thing. Until she stopped resisting. They hauled her upward. Toward the top of the ridge. All the while keeping up a patter, cajoling, soothing. You'll see him again soon, they said over and over. Don't worry. You'll see him again soon.

Ashley will never understand how her mother could leave him like that. Jimena knew—she had to know—that Rafael would be caught. She must have trusted that his captors would treat him kindly. Take him to a hospital to have his bone mended, leg set in a cast, then provide a safe ride back over the border. That from there he'd find his way home to Mexico D.F., and rest and heal and, when the time was right, return. That with the second attempt, the lessons of the faulty first try learned, he'd succeed. Cross desert, mountains, vast swaying tracts of *maíz*; ford rivers and lakes; and arrive at last in Nueva York, in Queens, where the young couple would reunite and face forward, toward their new life.

Mami, Mami, Mami—how often has Ashley yearned to take her by the wrists and scream into her moon-round face—how could you be so naive?

Because of course that's not how it went at all. It didn't matter how many times the brothers repeated as they hauled her upward that she would; Jimena would not see her husband again soon. Or ever. Not even when his body was in the morgue from where, if seven days passed and it remained unidentified, un-claimed, it would be delivered to the medical school for use as a training cadaver. She could not go to him where he lay cold and alone, sit by him, hold his hand, say farewell. If she did she risked being nabbed herself—everyone knew *La Migra* was everywhere in the border town—and flung away from the only future that remained for her. Fidel and Che, good boys whose mother had taught them well, stayed at her side, gently murmuring Honduran sayings of sympathy whose sweetness hurt her heart. They made her eat and drink. She swallowed what they put before her, steam-ing plates, *tamales*, *pollo*, *arroz*, cooked by kind local ladies they would never meet. She sipped at a bottle of beer the boys put to her lips saying it would help her sleep. She didn't sleep. The row of cots in the church attic where they hid with a half-dozen other recent arrivals rattled with snores, snorts, tossings and turnings, strangled cries through the night, and the narrow space was hot and dry so that her throat closed up, and it stank of farts and sour breath, but none of this was what blocked her sleep. The broth-

ers, and the priest too, Padre Alvaro—who took turns sitting with
Jimena, speaking to her in a low voice about the impossibility of
understanding God's plans, about Rafael's goodness, Rafael's luck
to now be in heaven with Jesus, telling her to rejoice for him, for
his happy afterlife now well begun—the three of them, Che, Fidel
and the priest, alternating shifts with her, prompting her to eat,
drink, brush her teeth, persuading her that, no, she must not go to
where they held her husband's body. The risk was too great. If she
were sent back they would neither of them have made it, and how
would that help his father in D.F. who had asthma and no job and
scrambled to survive? Or her brothers and sister in Puebla, where
there was no work for *campesinos* any more since NAFTA and corn
prices had risen so high whole days passed with only beans to eat,
not a single tortilla to hold them? All of them counting on, waiting
for, holding their breath until the money from *El Norte* began to
arrive.

They were right, the padre, the boys. She knew this. But how
could she bear to lose him without even the chance to say goodbye? Ashley has heard the tale a million times. From her mother, in
short spurts, sometimes the climb, sometimes the dogs, sometimes
the brothers, the debt she owes to Che and Fidel although she
supposes she'll never know what became of them, sometimes the
parting from Ashley's father, the scene there on the mountainside,
the wrenching wrongness of it, even then she knew, Mami has told
Ashley, at that very moment as she let the boys haul her away, she
felt it as an undeniable truth that she would never see her husband
again. So why did you do it? Ashley has always wanted to ask,
look what happened, you were right, he died, but she never has.
She couldn't hurt her mother like that.

The rest of it Mami has not told her. But Ashley has heard.
Nights when she was supposed to be deep in slumber, and she was,
but suddenly snapped awake. She'd think it was an elbow to her
side from her cousin Ofelia, or maybe on the opposite edge of the
bed Ofelia's younger sister Megan had kicked out in her sleep, but
then she'd realize it wasn't anything Ofelia or Megan did. It was
Mami's voice. On the other side of the wall in the kitchen, Mami
speaking steadily, a slurred monologue spiked by frequent shrieks
of "*ay Dios*" or "*los perros*," and Ashley knew that, as happened now
and again, Mami had stayed up drinking tequila with Tía Dahlia
so that Ashley's aunt could do Ashley's mom the service of listen-

ing once more to the terrible details, the unspeakable details except when her tongue was limbered by the liquor of the aguave tree, of how Ashley's father had died.

Jimena, Fidel, and Che had met Señor Estes' partner, Señor Contreras—"Call me Fermin," he said jovially, looser, less stern than his counterpart on the other side—at the top of the ridge as planned. This gentleman, experienced professional that he was, had already as he awaited their arrival ascertained that there were a number of *Migra* agents and their dogs in pursuit. He'd followed the quartet's progress, and the trackers', peering through powerful binoculars, prepared to hop into his four-by-four, speed down the dirt track and disappear into the city night leaving his charges to their unfortunate fate if it should prove necessary. He saw Rafael trip. He watched the others lift him, the effort to move on together, he saw the injured man sit, the few minutes of furious argument, and then how only three moved on. He was satisfied with their progress once the two lads managed to place the girl firmly be-tween them and hold her to their swift pace. When the threesome reached him, he proffered a bottle of water to each, then "*bueno,*" he said once they'd tipped the plastic to their lips, and "*vámonos,*" and he hustled them into the vehicle. He had been contracted to transport four people yet he did not ask why there were only three. He knew, Jimena has told Dahlia. He was watching while we made our way up, he was above us, he must have seen. But he said nothing.

What should he have said? Tía Dahlia always asked. Wel-come to *los Estados Unidos*, and by the way, *Señora, su esposo está muerto*? Begging your pardon, Missus, but I thought you'd like to know I just watched those devils set their dogs on him? Now please get into my truck and we'll begin the next leg of your jour-ney?

He—we—could have saved him! Jimena would reply, and Dahlia would sigh and say, "*Ay, m'hija,* who do you think you were, some kind of superheroes? They had guns, remember? They had dogs." Then Jimena would scream, "*Ay! Los perros!*"

And Ashley, lying between her cousins on the other side of the plasterboard wall, would get the weirdest feeling. A sliding sting from her gullet to her feet. A sort of guilty, sort of thrilling ping like a taut-strung guitar string vibrating along the length of her, lifting her like a high note out of bed and through the roof, zooming her westward out of Queens, over the East River, Manhattan and the Hudson, across the continent, zap, just like that, breaking the time barrier too, landing in Arizona on that night thirteen years ago and swooping down to save the day, slap, bam, pow, outmaneuvering the evil border agents and their frothing hounds from hell, lifting her father, her mother, and those good-natured Honduran brothers Fidel and Che, and spiriting them all back to the life they were meant to live, here, now, the 21st century in Corona, Queens. Where *tortillerías* line Roosevelt Avenue and taco trucks parked at the corners draw lunchtime lines 10 deep and if these *sabores deliciosos* aren't enough to stanch the homesickness that perfuses them, running thin and constant as hemophiliac blood, well then they can watch Channel 41, 47, 53, 67, 68, 69 or any of the four public-access stations to join familiar sights and sounds to the familiar tastes and smells that surround them here in the place that they, after all, they, Mami and Papi and all the others, chose as their destination. As she rescues them in her fantasy, Papi from death, Mami from the sadness that will henceforth flavor her days, Ashley always wants to remind them: this is your choice, you know. No one's forcing you. Turn back if you've changed your minds. Above all, whatever you encounter from here on out, don't blame me. I won't have the easiest time of it either. You might spend the rest of your lives pining for your homeland, but at least you'll always have one. What will I have? A weird mix-up of a name—I mean, Ashley Rafaela Dominguez Vargas? Mami, what were you thinking?—and plus which, Tía Dahlia isn't even my real aunt, she's just some lady you met when you first arrived who took pity on your poor pregnant self and took you in, and to top it off her kids Ofelia, Megan, and Sean aren't really hers, they're her sister's who died of diabetes right after she gave birth to Sean and so their dad, my Tío Sergio, not only isn't actually my uncle but he's also not my aunt's husband either, all of which explains why we four females sleep crammed into two beds in the only bedroom while Tío Sergio and Sean share the fold-out in the front room, not that Tío Sergio is here very often to sleep, working three jobs in Manhattan—and on top of all this weirdness there's you, Mami, clinging to me with your endless love and your permanent pain and confusion, and your inability or unwillingness to learn English so that I have to accompany you every year to the parent-teacher conferences and interpret what my teachers have to say about me, which I'm not supposed to hear, Mami, it's supposed to be between them and you, but there I have to sit, so embarrassed I could die, and listen to them, like this last time, Ms. Bernfeld, with her squinty green eyes magnified behind thick glasses so she always looks intense and surprised, going on and on about what a lovely child Ashley is, you should be very proud of her, Ms. Dominguez, Ashley's so smart such a good reader but so shy and how I should speak up more in class and all that, while you nod as if you know what she's saying, sitting stiffly upright, holding your purse tightly on your lap, biting your lip and looking shyly to the side, waiting till I repeat my teacher's words, doing the best I can to explain what she said in your language that will never be my own.

Ashley's consciousness always came crashing back to reality as her mother's cries of *"los perros! los perros!"* rose in volume and intensity and then, no matter how she tried, she couldn't remove herself back to her southwestern superhero mission to the past, couldn't block out the rest of the story Mami would never stop telling. How she and the brothers were dropped off in the city at the agreed-upon corner. How they paid Fermin the rest of the agreed-upon sum. How he pointed them toward the church on the edge of downtown where they could rest and hide until they were ready to proceed to wherever it was they aimed to get to. The three of them shook his hand, thanked him. He gave a funny courtly little bow, made a stilted little speech about wishing them well in achieving all their dreams here in this land of riches, and drove away.

They heard the next day. Someone in the attic had a radio tuned at low volume to a local Spanish-language station. The gruesome tale topped the news: several college students out on a rock-climbing day trip had found a body four miles out of town. A male, so mangled, what little skin remained hanging off his face and torso in strips, the sinew underneath reduced to bright red stew meat roasting in the desert sun, so defiled that it would be nearly impossible to identify him. Not that anyone was expected to try. He had no doubt been alone, some poor soul so desperate to make a new life that he'd attempted the crossing on his own. He'd made it surprisingly far, the reporter commented, but he'd been no match for the elements. A mountain lion attacked, perhaps; or perhaps beasts set upon his body only after he succumbed to thirst and starvation. If the young hikers who found him had come along an hour or two later there might have been little left but bones. It was the stink, steaming from whatever the grunting, gobbling turkey vultures were feasting on, that drew their curiosity. Once they realized this was human carrion, once they recoiled, gagging, once they caught the blond track star whose knees buckled and gave him water and revived him from the faint, they moved back toward the scavengers and jumped and yelled to drive them off. Three of the hikers stayed there protecting the corpse while the other two hustled back up the ridge and down to the access road and drove toward town to find the sheriff's office. The deputies arrived fast. Soon reporters were on the scene. The news hit the radio. A lone *indocumentado*, crossing the desert, had been set on and torn to pieces by wild animals. Poor man, the people in the church attic said. Shaking their heads. Crossing themselves, sharing looks that said any one of them could have been that unlucky *pobrecito*.

Jimena, Che, and Fidel immediately knew. This was no lone unfortunate—not until the end, *ay Dios*. The animals that killed him or, who knows, merely left him for dead, were not wild, at least not in the zoological sense. But they would never be identified, any more than their victim would be. And they would never be held accountable.

❀ ❀ ❀

Ashley doesn't remember her father but she cannot forget the reason she never met him. Not with Mami *"ay ay ay"*ing in the kitchen to Tía Dahlia on those occasional endless nights. As for the rest of her mother's own story, Ashley knows it in vague outline. How Jimena got the hell out of that *pinche* state with its *pinche* Grand Canyon into which if there were any justice the entire *pinche* Border Patrol, two-legged and four-, would fall to their painful, bloody deaths, five times more painful and bloody, no, ten times, than Rafael's. (One morning when Ashley was 9, walking home along 37th Avenue from Our Lady of Sorrows, her mother had taken her hand and confessed to her that vengeance, the more violent the better, was what she prayed for to *La Virgen* every Sunday before mass when she lit a candle and knelt and should have been asking Our Lady to watch over the soldiers in Iraq, or bless the fundraising campaign to bring in $17,000 to pay the Peragallo Pipe Organ Co. of Paterson, N.J., to repair the church's grand old instrument, or any one of several other intercession requests suggested by Padre Healy in his strange Irish-accented Spanish.) Jimena made her way to Queens, as planned, but she never found Emilio. Rafael's cousin's address had been in his pocket and they'd both forgotten about it in those final frantic minutes on the mountain. Twice she waited in line at a crowded call center to phone the auto shop in her village, first to leave a message for her sister, then to receive her sister's reply, that they hadn't heard from Emilio in two months, his cell phone didn't answer, letters had bounced back stamped "no such addressee." Still she'd somehow believed she could ask around—the neighborhood was known as *Puebla York* after all, surely someone would know Emilio Dominguez, the fast talker with the lightning-struck white slash down the middle of his black hair, the gap between his front teeth that always shows because he always smiles, Emilio who'd sent some precious pesos home and spent some on monthly calls extolling the virtues of life up north, urging his *primo* to join him. Emilio, you know, he drives a black car. Oh, he drives a black car, people would chuckle, do you know how many black cars there are on the streets of Queens, how many grinning boys hustle their way into the driver's seat only to lose the ride and all their money to the limo company that swindled them out of every centavo they'd saved?

So. No Emilio. Mami must have spent some hard days. Ashley doesn't like to picture the specifics. How she ate, where she slept. Jimena shy scared young hungry, front just beginning to bulge. Until she got up her nerve and started going into restaurants asking if she could work. Cook, sweep up, anything. After three failures, Mami meeked her way into the fourth place. As she whispered her request to the lady behind the front cash register, there, waiting for her takeout order, stood Tía Dahlia. Whose chest felt tight that night, one week before the anniversary of her dear sister's death which would also of course be Sean's first birthday, which was the real reason she was there, she'd just ordered the food for the party, half ashamed worried her sister in heaven would think she was too lazy to cook the feast herself but half certain she'd know it just showed the state of Dahlia's cracked-open heart, how she could carry everything, the joy and also the grief, she could accept even what she'd have once predicted would be unacceptable, the end of mourning, the mandate to go on, what everyone said, you've got to go on, go on, it's like the national slogan up here where no one lets you take the time to steep in sadness until it naturally recedes, still she could do it all except the one impossible thing. The kitchen alone. Always it had been the two of them, side by side. Pounding the *masa*. Rolling tortillas. Stirring the beans. Dahlia and her sister a team. And so although she could proceed, she could celebrate even, her nephew a year old, she could not cook. *Pues*, there she stood, the party order complete, waiting for tonight's takeout, a payday treat for Sergio and the kids, and she felt something brush past her ear. The slightest displacement of air. Jimena whispering, her nearly silent plea, *por favor, señorita*, let me sweep, in return only a little something to eat.

Ashley in her mind liked to simulate a drum roll at this point, or like maybe a brassy trumpet honking: ta da! ta da! The fateful meeting of Jimena and Dahlia! The start of the rest of everything.

How Dahlia took Jimena aside. Asked her story. Touched the girl's belly. How her palm remembered her sister, same bump, two years ago almost. And the coming anniversary, and her tender chest, and this poor lost girl's swelling breasts straining against her blouse. All of it a lucky circumstance for me, Ashley's mother has always said, which she always follows with an apology, to Dahlia if she's there, to God if she's not, for she would surely never imply that there was any luck in Dahlia's sister's death. But. Somehow. Same restaurant, Los Mismos Amigos, to this day their favorite, on Roosevelt at 103rd Street, same moment, what are the odds, it seems as though it was meant to be.

Dahlia took Jimena home. Jimena and Dahlia cooked and cleaned and slept side by side. Jimena helped with the kids. Jimena had Ashley. Dahlia found her a job, early shift to balance her afternoons, and Jimena joined the crowds boarding beat-up vans every morning at 6. Crossing eastward out of Queens to work alongside 17 other women packaging air fresheners in a factory in Nassau County.

Safe and free.

Until last month.

Thirteen years in this country. Twelve years making a wage, paying taxes, Social Security, yes, in someone else's name, but what's the harm, that lady's long dead, Jimena has never claimed a benefit and she's worked every day hard as anything. Hard as every night dreaming of everything she left behind. Her family. Her home. Those twin little hills across the arroyo beyond which the sun rose every day in a spectacular purply thrill as if to announce,

Buenos Días, everyone, have no fear, I am here once again. Thirteen years she's been not homeless, thanks to the goodness of Dahlia, long since like a sister, not homeless strictly speaking yet for all this time without a home. This is how she's lived. An in-between. For Ashley. And now they tell her she has to go.

They don't call it *La Migra* anymore. ICE is what it is. Immigration Control and Enforcement. ICE like death. Like no feelings. Blood frozen in their veins, it must be, to do what they do. What they did. Last month.

They took all 18. The boss wasn't there that morning. Everyone thought it odd but who would think to question, sick aunt, they were told, he'd be back in a day or two, and it's not as if they needed him, hell no, in fact it was a relief, him not hovering over them hissing hurry up hurry up. They could run this place with their eyes closed practically. So, funny thing, that morning at first seemed practically a holiday. Jimena and the rest working steadily but chatting, too. Someone even propped the back door open so there was a nice little breeze. Perfect day for it. April. The world warming a bit. Until almost lunchtime. When everything exploded, cold.

Screeching tires, doors slamming, jangling metal clanging against itself, and fast as anything in runs an army of black-clad crewcut shock troopers, and they're waving guns and shouting, "Homeland Security!" and "Nobody move!" and "Papers! Papers!" and they're jumping up on the tables and turning off the machines, knocking people around, one of the women cries out as she falls and lands on her elbow, a few try to weave between the raiders and duck out the back door but they tumble right into more of them, a line of black-suited baseball-capped *falangistas*, feet planted apart, M16s thrust forward and it's all over fast, 18 women cuffed, shoved into three lines, chain-ganged, shackled at ankles and wrists each to the one in front, pushed up into vans and driven away.

Fifteen minutes tops, and Jimena was gone.

When Ashley got home from school half the block was out on the sidewalk. Half the moms had been nabbed in the raid. Little kids crying, bigger ones trying to comfort them, lots of yelling and cursing, the Channel 41 truck rolling up, but all Ashley wanted to know was how, how could it happen, why was there no warning, why couldn't Mami have missed her ride that morning and most of

all why take her? What was her crime? Working? Caring for her
daughter? Walking down the street always with her head a little
down, never leaving Queens in her entire life since she arrived
except for her Long Island job? Spending her nights hearing again
and again the dogs? Tía Dahlia said it must have been the boss.
Sick aunt, right, sure, he knew in advance, they'd told him to stay
away, and what does he care, that *cabrón*, that *hijo de la chinqada*,
tomorrow he'll hire a whole new crew.

It took most of the rest of that first week—the raid on a
Monday and not till Wednesday when some volunteers from a little
storefront office in Jackson Heights who said they were for immigrant rights came around and then Thursday when they called
with the information they'd found out—until Ashley knew where
her mother was. The ICE Detention Center in Elizabeth, New
Jersey. The Jackson Heights people said Jimena's 17 co-workers
were scattered all around, some in county jails, some in the Wack-
enhut Detention Center here in Queens, but Mami—Mami was in
a whole other state.

Ashley waited. For Tía Dahlia to figure out a way to get a
lawyer, in between working and worrying and checking Ashley's
homework as she always has because her English is pretty good
and cooking Ashley's favorite food and promising her that Mami
would be back soon. For Mami to call, which every TV show says
you have a right to do when they arrest you so why didn't she?
One little phone call, Mami's voice in her ear so she could hear
she's still there. Still here. In the same country at least. Which has
never been Ashley's mother's country. Ashley's neither, not really,
even if it's all she knows, because what else she knows is that if
she asked Tía Dahlia for two dollars and bought a Metro card and
rode that #7 train into Manhattan for the first time in her life, and
got out and walked along the famous 42nd Street everyone would
look at her like a freak, like a foreigner, how could they not, she's
not from this place even though she is, it's in her face, anyone can
see, and even if she didn't encounter anybody truly mean, even if
no one shook a nasty finger at her and told her to go back home
where she belongs, she'd know they were thinking it and she'd
know there was no such place. No home. No belongs.

About a week after they took her mother away—a week of
sitting in school with her head on her desk thinking about never

seeing her mother again, or else her mother being deported to Mexico and sending for Ashley to join her there, swallowing down the empty panic at the first, life without Mami, but then having trouble breathing at the other, leaving for a strange new land—Ashley's English teacher Ms. Bernfeld asked her would she go downstairs to the library with her after last bell. She had Ashley pull up a chair so they could share a computer station. She said that even though she didn't teach history or geography, she knew a little bit about each and asked would Ashley mind surfing the web with her. She started typing words Ashley didn't know, like "pre-Columbian" and "indigenous," pulling up maps, charts, timelines, all these crazy websites with names like *"Reconquista"* and *"Primero de Mayo"* and who knew what. She told Ashley that if she wanted, they could come down here every day after last bell and look at this stuff. That she might learn something that would help her understand the context for her mother's arrest. It was the first good feeling Ashley had had since they took her mother, that Ms. Bernfeld assumed she knew what she meant by "context."

After two more weeks she started to see it, like the scenery behind what was happening onstage. How this land had once been full of people who looked like her mother and her. How it had been theirs. Stolen, some people said. The gringos are the foreigners, they said, not us. There were groups that were trying to stop the ICE raids. There was even going to be a march. If Ashley wanted to go, Ms. Bernfeld said, she'd give her a subway map and show her how to get to Union Square.

One day Ms. Bernfeld said she had to grade some papers and Ashley should go to the library on her own. Ashley Googled "Jimena Vargas de Dominguez Treviño." Lots of Vargases came up. Dominguezes, Treviños. And Jimenas. But there was not a single citation for her mother's full name. All those years of stepping so quietly through Queens: Mami had left no trace. Ashley ran to the bathroom and threw up. She sat on the floor of the stall for a long time. Ms. Bernfeld could show her a hundred websites proving it was the whites, not Ashley, who were the foreigners, but not even a thousand would fill the Mami gap in Ashley's insides.

Eventually she got up. She washed her face. She went back into the library to log out. The search engine shone onscreen. She Googled her own first name.

Ashley: 122 million citations.

She could scroll through the list for a year and barely make a dent.

Yet that's what she started to do. In the library after school. Every day. She Googled Ashley. Acquainted herself with some of her namesakes. She skipped past the fan sites for the stars, like the Olsen twin and Ashley Tisdale from *High School Musical.* She concentrated on Facebook and most of all on MySpace, where there were tons of Ashleys. Many were teenagers and college kids, but some were around 12 like her. Lots of them were white, but lots weren't. There was an Ashley who'd been born in China but now lived with her two mothers on the Upper West Side, a Dominican Ashley in Washington Heights, an African American Ashley in Detroit and another in an Atlanta suburb, and lots and lots of Mexican and Guatemalan and Salvadoran Ashleys, all over the place, Queens and Westchester and Freehold, New Jersey, and Bakersfield, California. She didn't have her own email account; they weren't allowed to create a MySpace page from school; there was no computer at home. Which meant she couldn't join any of the chat rooms or IM any of the Ashleys. So she contented herself with moving through the public pages, privately meeting the Ashleys one by one.

She sat at a computer in the I.S. 61 library from 2:30 to 4:30 every afternoon of the third and fourth week after ICE took her mother away. Scrolling through page after page of Ashleys. The most peculiar notion started to run through her mind. My space. This carrel, this chair. This Leonardo da Vinci School and this 50th Avenue. Corona, she thought: this is my space. She heard herself think it and she knew it was kind of whack but it wouldn't stop, it was filling her head. My space: Queens. My space: New York. My space, Mexico—this was a test, a leap, she could fall, she could crash, but she didn't, she heard herself think it and she knew it was right and in her mind she started to soar—my space my space my space my space. It made her grin for the first time since the raid. She pictured marching with the people against ICE next week, taking the train—why not? the train was her space too!—marching for Mami and chanting. She made up a goofy chant: "This space is my space! This space is my space!" And maybe it wasn't so goofy, maybe everybody would say it with her, maybe it would be like all the Ashleys carried across the globe by moms, adoption, war, hunger, history, all of them were marching alongside her. She and all the Ashleys in the world shouting, "This is my space! This is my space! This is my space!"

It wouldn't fill the Mami hole, Ashley knew. But it was a good, true thought, and maybe it would hold her for a while.

Mark Weiss, photograph

Sleeping in the House of Saints

Don't you want to ask —

Why must the wife of the santero *wear
earrings made of earth and wood?*

By day, his women balance silence.

In the *nicho, la Guadalupana* wants
the sun, stands above the moon.
Hers is the cloak of cold heaven,
crown of December pearls. How beautiful
su mandoria, body halo tipped *almagre*
through topaz heart of flame. *Mira*:

Our Lady of the Rosary: He has carved *her*
out of cottonwood, entwined the child
with its roots. The sadness of her face.
The robe spinning ribbons and veins.
She cradles the kneeling world
between candles and rainbow of God.

By night, in the chapel of their bedroom,

the wife of the saint-maker is unveiled,
a ruby at her center. His fingers sculpt
her hair to juniper, skin gessoes
to his touch. Paradise. This, and then, this:
She is the perfumed altar of midnight.
He is the deepest moment of dark.

Don't you want to ask —

*What must our lady suffer to wear
earrings made of blood and stars?*

doña luz cannot fly

in the old courtyard, right of the plaza,
los guerejos flock and feather about her

doña luz loads fruits into her basket
persimmon   jackfruit   lemon

colors form a triangle like gloves
of flame trees off malintzin

now freckled eggs, green-blue marked
with brown, lard and beans, lavender

for the jug with a crack of lizard's tail,
red-chile *ristra* and *tomatillos*   green

like her loneliness   wind on her face
pricks like claw prints of the hill-crow

doña luz pulls her cape of midnight

about her   raven-cloth wings to lift

her to a tiny house with red shutters
and the tin beak for a doorknocker

inside windows born of ebony and dirt
her skywash shadow shifts dusk across

walls of moon-bleached lizard bones
y entre dos luces sapphire lady threads

fire of rag sage and string berries   listens
to owl-silence nesting in corners of her life.

Alice Lindsay Price, pencil, copyright 2001

Speaking River

hold your mouth shut
and you bring the river into you

> odd that water would behave
> hostile to breath, and pregnant —
> > gar, green bloom, cyclops,
> fugitives afraid to open throats to sun

I used to be you, declaiming
> working the jowls
> muscle my brown protest out

easier to expel than imbibe
> saying without saying

I discovered the back of the teeth
muting the water's spine
> no allegiances

cutting the river root
with the tip of a folded tongue

from *There Is a River: El Paso / Juárez*

Perhaps I first felt the abeyance on the bridge's yellow
stripe demarcating the boundary between the United States and
Mexico. Above me, stars and stripes, eagle and serpent, snapped
in the wind and azure heat of August; beneath me trickled the Rio
Grande, or Río Bravo, depending upon which side of the border
one learned geography. A strange feeling, for all of the words I had
used to define myself until then were what they, the schools, my
parents and friends, had contrived to indicate skin color, religion,
water, bread, sadness . . . .

The traffic continued. Jalopy radios blared *norteño* drug-traf-
ficking ballads, brakes squealed, engines hissed and rattled, the
whole pulmonation of thousands of workers and tourists clogging
the lanes into El Paso, into the United States, into the same desert which seamlessly spread its sands across languages and laws
in one scalding, indifferent blaze. But I was ignorant even of the
pedestrians who passed me, Americans with plastic bags of tequila
and leather *tchackis*, Mexican youths on their way to the mall,
grandmothers carrying bags of *tamales*, soldiers on leave. If I had
listened, I would have heard the cathedral bells in the plaza by the
mercado, the train's howl and clack on rails crisscrossing from the
state of Chihuahua into Texas, and the loudspeakers from redbrick
warehouses jumbled across the edges of El Paso. Yet I heard nothing but my slowed breathing, while my fingers clutched the chain-
link fence through which I gazed into the shards of cinderblock
neighborhoods, concrete banks below splattered with spray-paint:
US fuera de Iraq, Quiero con juan gabriel, La biblia es la verdad leela, as
well as cluttered streets of discount stores and shoppers milling
around downtown El Paso, the Victorian homes of Sunset Heights,
and the highway that connects two coasts, yet not before streamlin-
ing through this desert.

I realized my name was misleading when neighbors in Juárez
noticed my skin color as I opened my door to the streets of *la
colonia bella vista*, when Anglos from the Southwest looked at me
suspiciously and inquired about my background, or when others
with names brimming over with the Sabbath wine of Odessa called
me "Side-man," as if I were a character to the left of everything
they thought center, or the accompanist to some wild saxophone

solo they couldn't hear. That I was raised speaking the wrong
language. That I had no parents because, being adopted, I had
too many, or that they all were equally my estuaries. And that if
I were to start searching, the search would start in that city first
named as a mere pass between mountains, and then re-named after
a president of Zapotec blood, because it was as far from Sherman
Oaks as possible, and, if my God were to be a hoarse desert deity,
let him appear in a border-town between yes and no, between *no*
and *sí*. Let him grow brown and sinewy in that teetering between
abundance and paucity.

That pause couldn't have lasted long. I was always tired from
the walk back into Juárez, a three-mile hike from the university.
My shirt would have been dyed dark blue from sweat. The rest of
the way was down the bridge and into the streets lined with drink-
and-drown bars, strip clubs, steaming taco stands, and stray dogs.
And if I were to see Maricela that afternoon I would have been in a
hurry. (Maricela of the narrow, rose-bud breasts. Maricela of the
milk-soft smile.) I would have asked someone in Spanish for the
time, and that pedestrian would have paused and asked, *¿La hora de
Juárez o de El Paso?*, an hour difference. And could I respond now,
I would state: *Neither*. For it was always neither.

On the first afternoon we were to spend together, she told
me to wait for her around noon in front of the *Noa-Noa* on *Avenida
Juárez*. Waiting in Mexico is a relaxed affair, a bouillon cube dis-
solving in bubbling water. Everyone arrives 15, 30, or 40 minutes
late, like some slow prophecy, like the messiah who, according to
Kafka, arrives on the day after one needs him. One sits at a bar
and stares at the white-vested *cantineros*, or watches the traffic pass
by, as I did. Car after car inching up the avenue to the international bridge. Glaring heat, and the piercing police whistles directing
traffic, and the drivers honking their horns. *Mar-i-cela*, I repeated,
a name awash with sunlight and sea. One can stand on the avenue
and wait and not get bored: mariachis wandering up and down the
avenue; the ambulatory shoe-shine with his case of oily rags, polish, and his groaning of *¡Boleo! ¡Boleo!*; the sight of an American in
his mid- twenties standing on the sidewalk, waiting.

"Wait for me in front of the Noa-Noa," she told me, "and I'll
be there at noon."

Now, under the white sunlight, I had to confess: "I've no
money."

She smiled, it was on her, and as we walked down the avenue, it was obvious how we must have met, how incongruous we were. We walked drunk with heat, radiant with the candor the young possess for a short time before it's snuffed out by convention, by middle age.

❊ ❊ ❊

Stretched over the international border, a border that is liquid and has shifted its course several times, the Santa Fe Street Bridge connects two cities that seem to have been joined only for economic convenience. Downtown El Paso is a dusty sprawl of side streets and stores selling everything from kitchenware to perfumes for under a dollar. Boxes stuffed to the point of splitting with socks, t-shirts, or clock radios crowd the sidewalks where Korean hawkers and their help, young women from Juárez, shout out their litany of *Pásale, barato barato* and *Ésole, pásale jóven*. On weekends, families from the unpaved *colonias* of Juárez wait for up to three hours to cross the bridge, and then walk those streets, despite the omnivorous sunlight. Their bags of booty, Chinese toys, blue jeans, swap-meet gold, that *sea-horde of deciduous things*, are what keep that oldest section of El Paso thriving.

The same bridge spills into downtown Juárez, a section abandoned by the lower and upper middle class, except for some of the university students who, during their brief flirtation with bohemian culture, frequent the ruinous bars. There—a few blocks from the strip—commence the poorest *colonias*. Gangs, family-owned grocery stores, stray dogs, children playing with blown-out tires and firecrackers fill streets that press up against the main strip. By night, the *Avenida* attracts underage drinkers from Las Cruces, El Paso, and Ysleta, as well as men who visit the brothels and strip clubs, like the one where Maricela worked, hustling drinks, and dancing with a bored sway on a tiny stage to the same songs by The Eagles and The Doors. By day, afternoon tourists wander through the arts and crafts stalls with their velvet paintings, ponchos, and statuettes of cacti and dozing men doomed by their sombreros, while the locals stay indoors, seated in front of their fans.

There is no other border traversed by so many on a daily basis, no other international bridge crossed by hundreds of thousands each day; there is no other bridge which so clearly embodies the function of a bridge: to connect, yet also to make distance, or boundaries, emblematic. Commerce, illegal and legal, uses this five-lane route where overheating cars, bike riders, and pedestrians on the walkways slowly wend to work, family, classes, lap dances, shopping, a ripping off of Protestant restraint, a stable paycheck *en oro*, dollars, not *plata*, by cleaning offices, frying burgers, changing tires.

A violet region that resembles dawn or dusk, and, in actuality, is neither.

An estuary.

Everything becomes tainted with everything else; the Spanish spoken on the ramshackle streets of *el FOVISSTE, el centro, la colonia bella vista, la alta vista, anapra* melds with English, and new verbs mushroom: *watchar, parquiar, desponchar*…. Or the syntax unravels in order to accommodate the coupling of verbs and prepositions in English: *volver p'atras* and *devolver p'atras*.

In El Paso, in the plaza where William Carlos Williams listened to the chatter of sparrows and stared at the toothless alligators in their caged pit, the men and women sitting on benches are brown-skinned, and spoon *elotes* mixed with salty cheese and *chile* powder into their mouths. Indeed, it almost seems as if one is in Latin America; almost . . . for there is only the merest hint of colors more festive, more conducive to the baroque, flickering over the pragmatic Anglo architecture.

In Juárez, Anglo-America starts before you cross the bridge into Texas; apart from the Arches and Fried Chicken, those avatars of globalization, mini-malls line wide boulevards that look like dismal stretches of Los Angeles, such as Sylmar, Pacoima, or Arleta. I would finish my classes at the university in El Paso, and then walk through the abandoned streets in the Sunset Heights district, pass the Interstate, make my way through the ever louder streets in downtown El Paso, until arriving at the Segundo Barrio, the edge of the United States where last century the curious watched the Mexican revolution and where there still stands the building, two blocks from the bridge, where exiled Mariano Azuela wrote *Los de abajo* (ironically translated into English as *The Underdogs*). The building now has a soot-covered commemorative plaque; through the open gate, you see laundry lines and the t-shirts and underwear of the current residents flapping in the breeze like signs of surrender.

By the time I walked down a narrow street bypassing the strip, it would be dusk. Within ten minutes, I would reach my block. In order to find relief from the heat, the women would be seated outside their houses, gossiping and picking pickled pork-skin and chips from plastic bags. Rising above the sound of brakes grinding, the downshifting of passing buses, or the barking of dogs, I would hear the laughter of children, and then the greetings: *¿Qui'huuuu-hole? ¿Qué pues, güero?*

I rented a house behind my landlord's place. His porch, the only one on the block, was filled every evening until ten o'clock or later with local men who wanted to drink brandy, brag, spit, and joke, freed from the tedium and nagging of wives. Sometimes I would stay and talk; Don Manny, my landlord, always had his drinking stories, and then at times Pájaro, a mentally retarded man-boy who wore knickers, would amble down the street and stop to serenade *boleros* to passing groups of teenage girls. *La Brazileña*, a transvestite who lived with a truck driver, would be opening up her corner beauty salon. Boys would play soccer in the middle of the street, the ball slamming against parked cars, and then they would disperse whenever a police truck would rattle over the potholes. Usually the men would insist that I sit down for a bit; there were always jokes to tell, and there was always enough in the bottle for everyone to share. *¿No quieres un traguito?*

James H. Young, *Viejo*, photograph

from *The Pozos Diaries*

Walking the high plains in this town, over old lava beds and fields of wildflowers, we discovered narrow dirt roads, perfect for pedestrians, bicycles, or one car at a time. To our great surprise, behind the rows of *maguey* plants and *mesquite* trees, there are cornfields abundantly flourishing. Here we are at the end of August, whose full moon cast a golden blanket over the tiled rooftops and stone streets. In most places I have lived, the end of summer means harvest, and in New Mexico, they would be harvesting and roasting green chile now. But this corn has just recently been planted, as it is only a few inches tall. It still feels surreal to live in a region with a year-round growing season.

On this walk we also discovered the ruins of a cemetery that looks like it hasn't been used in a hundred years or more. A *panteón*, it's called here, or sometimes, a *camposanto*, containing structures similar to bread ovens with six or eight oval-shaped openings. It reminds me of a film I once saw, in the Mexican Magical Realism genre, the opening scene of which began in a cemetery much like this one. A father was pulling his long-dead daughter out of one of these openings, and discovered that her skin was perfectly preserved and she smelled like roses.

In full bloom right now is the *nopal* cactus, whose bright cherry-red fruit is called *tuna*. In the *mercados* and along the roadside, these are sold as snacks, cut up in plastic cups and ready to eat.

Moctezuma's revenge returned and I had to take *antiparasito*. Neighbors across the street showed us a weed that grows here, Santo Nicolas, with which to make a tea for such problems. I started with that, then added tincture of wormwood and black walnut, and in less than a day, I was feeling better than I have in weeks. The water purification system has been completed, and everything from drinking water to clean water for dishes and washing vegetables is available right from the tap. The best part is how delicious it tastes, without that plastic flavor from bottled water.

I think we've cracked the code for the bell-ringing, after many sleepless nights trying to figure out what time it really is. At a quarter past the hour, two consecutive dingdongs, rather melodic, come before the strikes, which signal the hour. At half past, two sets of consecutive, followed by strikes; at three quarters past, three sets of consecutive; then at the hour, four sets, followed by the strikes that signal the new hour. Can you see why it took so long? Now there is an additional problem. Sometimes the burros repeat their hee-hawing mantras many times in succession, and in those quiet night-into-morning hours, that special time they call *la madrugada*, I find myself halfway between waking and sleeping, counting the burro calls.

Pozos, 2005

David Casas, photograph

Hello from the Hills of Oaxaca

> Where is the Duende? Through the empty arch enters
> a mental air blowing insistently over the heads of the dead,
> seeking new landscapes and unfamiliar accents; an air
> bearing the odor of child's spittle, crushed grass, and the
> veil of Medusa announcing the unending baptism
> of all newly-created things.
>
> — *Federico García Lorca*

I.

You taught me to remember this tide
of chicken feathers rising around
the windshield, falling back like a veil
and the hills in this half-light, women
lifting *maguey* skirts, pulling off cloud-masks;
their faces a flash of foam on a cup of cacao —
that beauty begins with a grease fire in
the eyes. Like dragonflies, we marry
the light. We injure ourselves, instinctively.

I study the codices in the museum —
the foreheads of Olmec infants flattened
with boards at birth, the obsidian prongs
widows used to pull out their own tongues;
their wailing an affect I can only imagine,
faith that one day the beloved will return
like a secretive snake in new skin.

II.

You taught me that we are afraid
most of the time to say our names,
to name the thing that's missing. I want
to crush this spine of stars tonight,
knowing that all life is being released
out there beyond the fractured cars
and the half-lives of houses, the apologies
and flea-bitten dogs. Out there
in the ancient murky dark —
a corkscrew opening on the bright, bleak
smell of copal and the rosary's Latin hiss,
like an engine that refuses to turn over.

81

Scenes from Mexico City

Traffic whirling at roundabouts, a man off to the side
trying to sell a chair. I'm after the artwork
of Kahlo and Rivera, the bit of culture I can pack
into four days. I stand in line to see
the Virgin of Guadalupe, passing the poor
in the square, trying to look away. One small girl
won't take her eyes off me. Nothing though
like the Parachute People, those who've landed
outside the city and can't find jobs, who live in huts
with corrugated roofs draped with bougainvillea
bright as the sun, no water for miles. On the ride
to Taxco, the bus driver stops to buy slices of cactus
from a vendor, and passes them out. I've read not to eat
fruit from stands, but can't say no. We have lunch,
and I'm seated with three women who don't speak English.
I eat the creamy flan in silence and remember
the restaurant I ate at the night before
where swans swam behind glass,
under an arched brick ceiling. Kahlo and Rivera
could have eaten there. God knows Diego,
large as his murals. And small Frida, who insisted
her paintings were not surreal, might have picked at something.
The last painting she did was of watermelons, the luscious red,
the pit-black seeds. At the center, a whole melon
reminiscent of those orbs you'd find in much of her work,
some haunting planet, some eye that never ceased watching.

Magnolias

After Frida Kahlo, 1945

in various stages of opening,
white shaded with cream,

arranged in a globe-shaped
vase decorated with stalks.

Sickly sweet smell in the heat,
petals that bruise to the touch —

already ants are feasting. That year
the artist wrote, *Not the least hope*

remains to me. Yet a flower
in the center, radiant with pistil

and stamen. One blossom could
easily fall upsetting the symmetry.

So fooled we are by the green
leaves and thick stems as if

they could go on supporting
this beauty forever.

Harley Manhart, *Magnolia*, photograph

Two Voices: Diego's Calla Lilies

—*after* Nude with Calla Lilies

Kneeling on a petate mat,
The basket, deep enough,
an Indian woman sits upright,
supports our long, firm stems.
her unclothed frame scented.
We settle into clots of dirt.
Is it sandalwood? Mahogany?
Like absinthe, we intoxicate
I paint her broad shoulders:
the artist who shapes the woman's arms
earthy dabs of nutmeg, hyacinth
with the mastery of sun
so she can thrive like the flowers,
so she can embrace us.
so she can feel the florets swell.
Her hands, smelling of freesia,
Soon, she will rise out of shadows
reach out to our trumpets blaring
to gather bluets, yarrows.
as though she hears a mariachi horn,
What is happiness, if not this need?
feels our desire to return to marshes,
See how she rests—a saint—holding
watery fields, shallow pools far from
pearls tamed like fire?
the lover who approaches a street vendor—
Now, maybe you understand who I am.
scissor snips ringing through the market,
In the city, in the valleys,
fleshy tubes and arrow-shaped leaves
I wander in search of legends
rolled into wrapping paper, sold for a few pesos,
to begin anew. Oh, these calla lilies!
the blooms' swanlike hearts pounding.

Halley's Comet

*In the Gallery of the San Carlos, Diego Rivera's first
one-man exhibition opened on November 20, 1910 —
the same day the Mexican Revolution broke out
with an uprising against the dictator, Porfirio Díaz.*

I.
You gloat at the Opening. Regal, prim,
the dictator's wife buys six paintings
and toasts your success. *The Valley
of Ambles* and *The Tranquil Hours*
belie the tension mounting outside
the city among *campesinos*. To think
that years later you would lie, claiming
you intended to assassinate Díaz,
claiming Lenin needed you abroad
to arbitrate among Mexican factions.
Could you not own up to the truth?
In May, I soared through skies over
Mexico, warned your countrymen
to heed the unrest. Some called my
fiery appearance an omen. You,
Diego, were in Paris. With an eye
averted, you painted long into night.

II.
Look at you, *muy importante*
in a tailored suit. Your bulging
eyes pierce holes into a critic
who barely notices your art.
Go ahead. Cast him off
as you later would Angeline,
who bore your son, and Marevna,
mother of the baby you labeled
child of the armistice. Do not
ignore me. Others before you

have been this careless. In 66 AD,
I steered ships off course.
1066, I flew over England,
cursed Harold of Hastings.
In the 1300s, I posed as Giotto's
Star of Bethlehem, curved
like a saber over the Nativity.
Each time I reappear, I make
a more powerful showing.

III.
Egotistical. Quarrelsome.
The devil is in the room, Diego.
Mask after mask you wear
like armor. As a boy you opened
the stomach of a pregnant mouse,
played with your brother's corpse
at a wake. What do you say now
to a child soldier who bears arms,
stumbles over bodies in barren fields?
How many etchings, drawings,
oils did you bring here to please
la crema de la sociedad?
In a corner of the gallery, patrons
surround one of your masterpieces,
admire the rotund face staring back.
You lift a glass to the hostess, guests,
to the long life of Don Porfirio.
How can you ignore the cries
of the dead rattling the windows
of this sumptuous hall?

Cities Held Aloft by Women and Dogs

1.
This time of year the monarchs bloom from trees and earth,
sumptuous walls of orange and wind like the chrysanthemums
sold in temporary markets outside the cemetery gates. When the bored children
of the flower-sellers erupt into their flower fights, flinging blossoms,
it can be hard to tell what is petal
and what is wing.

But that's down South.
Here in the cities just below
the border, the butterflies
came through over a week ago,
trudging past our second-story window,
keeping their distance from us
and from each other, barely within eyesight
in the slowest, most staggered line.

2.
The paintings of Rodolfo Morales show seated women dandling on their aproned laps
houses, *cantinas*, *abarrotes*, municipal halls. Or side by side, the matrons hold up
archways and town squares. Usually, as in real life, interested dogs look on.
There are seldom men. This last is an exaggeration. In real life, there are a few.
A new groom too in love with his wife to head North this year. The ghosts.
The arthritic. The little boys waiting for their turn to go, and also for their mustaches.
The cowboy-hatted hero of the soap opera, the one about tequila.

3.
Because *Dia de los Muertos* is when the monarchs appear,
it's long been said that the dead come back in their form,
but in these half-ghost towns the women have started to hope
that maybe the *only gone* do too, have started to wait
for the arrival of insects as for the mail, as though a letter will
flutter down with the passing, or as though the movement of the wings will
push a scent of sweat and frost and tobacco all this way.

What else could you expect from men who learned from butterflies,
who took from them a lesson that you go as many miles as you have to
and then maybe someday you make it home if you can,
just ahead of the cold?

Sería Delicioso

Yo quiero estar
donde estuve.
Contigo, volver.
—*Pedro Salinas*

Quisiera evocar un instante
de mi adolescencia.
Una noche, illuminada, en el *Bambú*.
¿Era ahí, o en el *Johnny's 88?*
No importa, el mes fue septiembre.
¿O tal vez octubre?
Bailaba con alguien
a quien no recuerdo.

Afuera, un ciclón imperial, voluptuoso,
gemía destruyendo,
la naturaleza.
Y yo, por estar dentro, bailando,
Me lo perdí.

It Would Be Delicious

> I want to be
> back where I was,
> with you, again.
> — *Pedro Salinas*

I would like to invoke a moment
of my adolescence.
One brilliant night, in *El Bambú*
Was it there? or in *Johnny's 88*?
No matter. The month was September.
Or perhaps October?
I was dancing with someone,
but who? I can't remember.

Outside, a majestic, voluptuous hurricane
was howling, destroying
the natural world.
And I, by being inside, dancing,
I missed it.

Translated from the Spanish by George Petty

Claroscuro

El sol, insoportablemente inquieto,
se tendía desde un extremo a otro,
para fecundar
la Isla.

> Lo increpe, iracunda:
> ¡Cómo exacerbas nuestro deseo!
> ¿Qué pretendes? ¿A quién buscas?

A ti.

¿Por qué? Si nos entendemos.
Yo te miro de frente.
No te tengo miedo.

> Eso crees,
> pero cuando sientes escalofríos
> y la sangre hierve,
> ¿no te regocija el aliento de la noche
> y que te muerdan las sombras?

Chiaroscuro

The sun, insufferably restless,
cruised from one end to the other
to inseminate
the Island.

> I rebuked him, angry.
> See how you excite our desire!
> What are you after?
> Who are you looking for?

For you.

Why? We know what we're doing.
I look you in the eye.
I'm not scared of you.

> You think so.
> But when you feel the fever
> and the blood boils,
> don't you delight in the cool of the night
> and how the shadows nip?

Translated from the Spanish by George Petty

Siadó' guíe'

Sicarú rindani gubidxa,
naga'nda; riguiñe ti bi huiini'
rihuinni gubidxa naxiñárini,
naxiñrini rucheeche xpiaani.

Cayaze bigote ruaa bizé,
ti xcuidi cabee nisa ne cutiipi,
guguhuiini' zuba íque le'
cuyubilú neza guipapa.

Nuu tu riasa ma' zecaa nisa,
ne nuu tu neza ra ñaa ma'ze'
nanda xi' que' ti xigabá,
zeyasa yu dé neza ze'.

*Pancho Nácar wrote in Zapotec, one of the indigenous languages of Mexico. His works are only recently being translated into Spanish and English.

Daybreak Flowering

With splendor, the day is born;
a cooling breeze flutters;
the eye perceives how the sun is reddened as
it unleashes its light.

By the pond, the blackbirds preen;
a boy, whistling, draws water;
perched atop the fence, a red-
plumed bird peers for someplace to flit off.

Some, upon awakening, fetch water;
others set off to the fields,
and with drinking gourd hanging from their shoulders,
they go, stirring dust over the road.

Translated from the Zapotec by Anthony Seidman

Woodcut, 15th century

Xandú' Yaa

Cayaca xandú' yaa stiu' yanadxí,
Stubelu'cha' zuba ndaani' yoo;
Neca zitu ra ba' napa' lii,
Chupa xquíri'lu' caguí lu bidó'.

Nandxó' ñanda ñune' lii xandú yaa,
Pa ñaca ndaani' xquidxe' nibeza';
Dunabé huaxa naná rácani naa
Ti zitu nuaa ne xquidxi binni nabeza'.

Pa ñuaa' ndaani' xquidxe' nugaanda' biyé,
Nicaa' bichiisa nuzuchaahui' ndaani' yoo;
Guirá' cuananaxhi ña'ta' lu bidó,
Ñaazi' gueza, nisa dxu'ni' nudiee'.

Guirá huna huiini' nidxiña ñacané,
Ca ni bidxaagu' nidxiña nudii ná';
Sica ti yoo, ra cayuutu' binni dé
Nihuinni ra yoo, casaca xandú' yaa.

First Offering

Today is the first visit from your soul;
though I am here in this house, you
are in a distant tomb; in memory
of you, I light two candles to the saints.

I would set a great offering
in your memory if I lived in my *pueblo;*
how it aches in these moments to be
alone, to live in a foreign land.

If I were in my *pueblo,* I would raise an altar,
and with sacred palm leaves, sew stars
to adorn the walls, and I would set fruit
and tobacco on the sacred table, and offer liquor.

And the women, they would come and help;
those who were your friends would offer their hands;
as in a home where there is corn to be ground you would see
how we devoutly prepare this first offering for your soul.

Translated from the Zapotec by Anthony Seidman

El Viaje

Later, calculations will seem cruel or stingy:
the tip, the blind man on the sidewalk.
A dog with no tail turns away,
his street straight uphill.
At the *pueblocito* bus stop
seven hours from Guadalajara
I wonder if I said aloud
what I was just thinking.
Hombre, that girl is gorgeous,
eyes an impossible November,
hair the dream life of an enchanted crow —
nest of midnight, golden eggs,
the cold fire of stars.
The passengers on the bus
wish they could dance with her
all night, the bus won't stop,
the ocean lies in ruins
beneath her feet, weather breaks
after fourteen days of rain. A red light
reveals the captain's cabin
of a fishing boat on the horizon.
Above the fish he desires
he remembers his wife's black hair.

Guanajuato, El Dia Antes de Salir

Keep in mind it is the water that is the moon
and not the woman.
Remember you are a gentleman and the hours
can burn you like the sun.
A little girl swings a broom
taller than she is. Dust takes my hair
in its fingers. The dog at the edge of the square
has renounced all faith for his domain,
a plain of stones. He lies on them willingly.
The moon in the afternoon,
sky like a bone in a dream.
The patience of birds on the wire above me
is like the roar of an ocean that
after a day you no longer hear.
Voices through the phone lines
are silent smoke.
Women are rinsing limp blue shirts
in the river, tempting the current,
not even tempted to let go.
Tomorrow the bus begins reliving
old quarrels beneath the *camionera* awning,
my life already half dream.

San Pancho

The night I got here
it had been raining for twelve years.
Tourists and *meteorologistas*
had returned to their neglected families.
Wine was expensive.
Children watched TV all day
for another language and the pictures.
When I asked for directions
they loaned me a boy who speaks English.
He told me I speak English well.
In some countries if you cook for yourself,
being a man, you will live forever.
But alone. The wind will open your windows.
These crickets climb an impossible mountain
every day.

My Aunties Take Their Leave

The first to shrivel up
was the bright sprout of Aunt Palmira.
One afternoon she told us "tomorrow
I'll not awaken," and she bid goodbye
to everyone, to her rabbits and her chickens,
and before the sun rose
she left her distinctive morning fragrance.

Next to leave us was
the ramrod stalk of Aunt Pilar.
Breath of rain, vegetable blood:
one day she disguised herself as a plant
and disappeared in a dense mountain cloud.
In her goodbye she left us
a green and passionate embrace.

The last to leave was Aunt Piedad.
She left one afternoon in June.
Sprouting wings and adorned with setting sun
she flew straight off
which is the best way
for escaping responsibilities.
She left us nothing.

Quién eres, que / Who are You; What

To Barrie Cooke, the most abstract of the figuratives

In this world we walk
on the roof of hell,
gazing at flowers.
          —*Issa, Robert Hass translation*

1. The demon

spreads his flightless,
fringeless
wings
strolling
along
a line of hedges
never glimpsed before
or smelled
much less
cultivated,
all but wild
to be discovered
inside his fire,
not the one
that illusion shelters,
that in this life
this only one
we must enjoy,
allow to brim,
to wash through with elation
and more elation
until it liquifies;
we must never
expose
the beloved
to such heat,
such a flame

licking at the water
until it reaches
its first boil
that only one.
And that's how hard it is.

2. *Beauty, a Truth*

And one finds a way
to be continually present
to thresholds, penumbras

umbras

certainties, fortitudes, customs
clearly
seen.

For example,
decorum, finesse,
subtleties
feckless as the words
used to define
the sounds of love,

mastoid apophysis

a bone that throbs
in a cataract
cantata
loosened from everything
discontinuous
with itself
disgorged

from a goldfinch.

Consider, for example,
what fate,

through someone else's virtue,
might bring out in you.
Much more consolation
than grief
or its plural:
incurable
relief.

3. Birthmark

The touch of a thumb:
only light and distance.

Palm against palm:
an intuited uncharted
universe.

Its lines,
Fortune's
lanes
devoid
of any Future.
Meanwhile they blabber on, they talk
their ears off:
there is a landscape in its fullness,
an impulse to meet
the exhaustion that suddenly
looms from the hills
to present
that garden
of signs within signs.

4. Multiplied and Invisible Angle

Perchance to dream.

From the wine-
colored depths,

inebriate, solitude-colored,
from their fluvial agonies
and their crossings,
emerges a human being
feminine and very mortal
from the start.

Features.
Characteristics
particular
to languages
or colors.

Ochres against whites,
hair against skin,
muscular weight
against the lightness
of a personal history,
banal;
watercolors that evaporate,
saltless tears.

And even so,
such a history
might soften
itself in oils:
so to be that wounded body
in the canvas
that portrays and elucidates
this underground,
this paradise.

Translated from the Spanish by Forrest Gander

from *Cenizas de un mapa / Ashes of a Map*

La niebla es lo que ayuda al alma a subir al país del cielo.
La niebla es lo que ayuda al alma a subir al país del cielo.
La niebla es lo que ayuda al alma a subir al país del cielo.
La niebla es lo que ayuda al alma a subir al país del cielo.

Fog helps the soul rise to the country of the sky.

Translated from the Spanish by A. S. Zelman-Döring with C. D. Wright

El desierto incendia mi cerebro. La piel amurallada del elefante reposa en el circo como un timbre postal de otro planeta. La carta está escrita en este tapiz de niebia y la puerta cambia de lugar con la lluvia más ligera. Este es el orden; anagrama de polvo. Este es el azar: anagrama de polvo. Apenas se dibuja el nombre que adivino, uno ventisca lo disuelve.

El oráculo está roto; la miel, derramada.

The desert ignites my brain. The Elephant's tight skin holds fast the circus like a stamp from another planet. The letter is written in this foggy tapestry and the door moves with the lightest rain. This is the order: anagram of dust. This is chance: anagram of dust. Barely is the name I guess at woven, a mistral dissolves it.

The oracle is broken and honey is spilled.

Translated from the Spanish by A. S. Zelman-Döring with C. D. Wright

Oda para quedarse

Rien d'autre
on'ecrit plus qu'un nom
sur un peau de sable
—*Jean Pierre Spilmont*

La ciudad es tuya: la tocas. Arrojas una piedra a su río y partes en tu mesa su pan tibio. La ciudad es mía: la toco. Está desnuda en la antigua estatura de su catedral. Late su rosetón como un órgano fundamental, un corazón de vidrio que rota en las estaciones precisas. Sales de la iglesia y das vuelta en la Rue de Fourcy y nos acompaña hasta el Sena una imagen del campo fotografiada por Ralph Gibson. La luz del sol te toca, nos toca. Vacías tu boca de palabras gastadas y me dices algo que nunca había escuchado. Algo que no se puede retener en la memoria. Sé que es un nombre o un tejido de sílabas, algo en un francés vertiginoso. Lejos de ahí la palabra escapa como un salmón de la red. Sé que apenas me acerque al agua volverá a mi boca y podré tocar las cosas, los puentes y ellos a mí y tú dirás algo sobre sus barcos. Y el río será la vena de un cuerpo, la aorta de una vieja victoriosa, Nuestra Señora de París.

Ode to Stay in Paris

> Rien d'autre
> on'ecrit plus qu'un nom
> sur un peau de sable
> *—Jean Pierre Spilmont*

The city is yours: touch it. Throw a rock into its river and break its warm bread at your table. The city is mine: touch it. Naked in the old reaches of its cathedral. A fundamental organ its rose window beating; a heart of glass breaking certain seasons. Leaving the church, turn on the Rue de Fourcy to the Seine, image of the countryside photographed by Ralph Gibson. The sun's light touches you, touches us. Empty your mouth of wasted words and tell me something I haven't heard before. Something that can't be retained. A name or a weave of syllables, something vertiginously French. Something like God's other name. Far from there, the word slips through like a fish. I know I was close. The water will come back to my mouth and I will be able to touch things, the bridges, and they me and you will say something about boats. And if we don't want again to forget that name that which is almost a dress, we ought to stay.

Translated from the Spanish by A. S. Zelman-Döring with C. D. Wright

Ave María: A Song in my Shower

"*Ave Maria, gratia plena . . .*"

Today, I woke up with an Ave María stuck in my throat.
I did not know what to do with it, so I undressed, went into the
shower, and set it free. I could hear my daughter asking herself out
loud why I was singing hymns. As far as she knew I had not been
to church since baptism, and I often prayed about the excesses
of religion and the tight grip it had on civilization since Eve gave
Adam knowledge (I mean, an apple). Yet, this morning, as I let the
water run down the drowsy path of my bare back, an Ave María
danced out of my lips, clouding the mirror with its sumptuous
notes.

I myself wondered what the Ave María was doing in my
head, blurring my secularized mind, when a voice interrupted:
"*Me estoy poniendo bella porque voy al baile. Me voy a bailar,*" I
heard Grandma's coquettish voice in my head. "I'm making myself beautiful. I'm going to a dance." I saw my cousin Leti behind
her, braiding the three strings of gray hair left over from her once
abundant mane, many moons ago. Then I heard Grandma singing.

"Ave María . . ." The notes trembled in my ears, taking me
back to other hymns—all those hymns I used to hate as a child,
when my mother would force me to attend the daily rosary back
home, in Mexico (it was the month of May, the month of Mary).
We had to attend church because we weren't like everybody else.
We were decent people. Worse yet, we were "decent women."

Part of being a decent woman back then (and there) meant
never singing. A decent woman did not sing because most songs
spoke of those things decent women do not talk about, such as
desire. Decent men may sing all they want. In fact, if they did not
care for singing, they had the option of having a favorite song.
Grandfather did not sing, but everyone knew that his favorite song
was "*La Malagueña.*"

Grandmother was culturally unable to like that song, or
any other song that spoke of desire. The *Malagueña* voice spoke of
wanting to kiss a lover's lips—"*besar tus labios quisiera, Malagueña
salerosa . . .*" "I wish I could kiss your lips . . ." Not only was
Malagueña desirable, but she was a woman who knew how to
move. "*Malagueeeeeeña salerosa . . .*"

No, Grandma was not going to sing such foolish notes. But *"La otra,"* "the other woman," did. She sang. Often.

La otra was Grandfather's other woman. And as everyone knew, when she bathed in the hot springs, the bathing hole where the entire town shared its skin-deep secrets, she bathed to the tune of the *Malagueña*. Perhaps, as she felt the water caress her nipples, she felt . . . loved.

But, Grandma, well . . . Grandma was a decent woman.

She wanted to sing too, mind you. She had music in her veins. It was not her fault. Women have veins too. And some women are . . . singers. She wanted to sing. That is why she sang all the hymns to the virgin that she knew. That is also the reason that, when Ave María knocked on the door of memory this morning, I let her into my shower. I let her notes touch me. Her caress was a caress Grandmother surely had felt. (My daughter would certainly understand my birthing religion).

Ave Mariiiiiiiia . . .

David Casas, photograph

La Virgen de Rosario

(Morenci, Arizona)

I was 27 or 28. I had a ruptured
appendix & I knew that I was going to die.
La Virgen María came for me. She's so
beautiful, *mija*. She just smiled at me
& stretched out her arm.
      She was gonna take me.
I said, *No madre, no me lleves.*
No me quiero ir porque mi hijo
me necesita.
      She lowered her head. Her belt
was a big white rosary. She floated
into my room. There was a lot of fog.
I didn't see a hospital, just her
coming to my bed.
      Then she went to the room
of a little old lady that I had been
praying for. She'd been operated.
La Virgen took that *viejita* & she
gave me back my life.
      That was fifty years ago.
And look how long I've lived!
The other day I said, *Virgencita*
linda, if you come, now, I'll go.
I'm ready.
      I don't know why people are
so afraid of death. I always say this:
There's two things that make you
a survivor—guts & faith.
They go hand in hand. That's why
      I'm still around.

(from the memories of Josephine "Josie" Perú)

Paloma Triste

. . . caught in inexplicable and giant inhalations, windows not made to bend swell outward, snap inward, without sound, without breaking; without sound, grit scourges glass, immensity swirls, enormity circles, seeking the way in, looking—can you believe it?—looking for a boy of twelve . . .

. . . but the tormenta de polvo *is only one of* las escenas recurrentes *that return to torment him, to loiter in the brain of man or boy—for he is never quite sure if he is the man dreaming the boy in the yellow bus or the boy anticipating the old man seated in the plaza which has yet to be laid out, yet to be built . . .*

. . . and after each lingering, persistent scene, his mind, of whatever age, is particularly clear, lucid; the order of events is as straightforward, as intelligible, as the events themselves . . .

Tomás wasn't sure, but he thought Paloma had noticed him first. Paloma sat near the front of the class with all those *gringa* girls. Among so many pale puffy shapes Tomás could hardly fail to notice her darkness, the *café*-colored neck he would close his eyes against and dream.

That is, he would if she would let him, or if he were weightless and invisible and still, or already more spirit than flesh himself. But she might not, and he wasn't; and so there was nothing for him to do but gaze at one bent, thinking head lost among lighter heads ballooning with kids' talk and ranchers' words, anti-poor, *antimexicano*, anti-government *palabrería*, air as hot and empty as that which lay along the *México, Nuevo México* border.

A narrow rivulet of fine hairs ran an inch or two down Paloma's neck before vanishing *como agua en las arenas*. And there were days when Tomás would rather contemplate them than be consumed in the unending glare from above, the blaze that made targets of them all if they but knew. Turning away from such brightness only spun whatever it was within him, whirlpool or whirlwind, *más y más rápidamente* until he was riding the walls of his own tensed body.

But a touch of his forehead to her neck and he would be, he was sure, *tranquilo, sereno*, and Paloma would realize *al instante* that they were really the only two learning anything in this class, a perception that would link them as certainly as if the two held hands every day after school and looked up at a map of *América del Norte* in a classroom emptied of *imbéciles*.

A boy and girl ultimately free to discuss the nature of sunlight or turbulence and tumult, of confusion and chaos, of revolution, of dust storms and the history of the world or anything else. Of the border, *por ejemplo*, and of two destined never to speak.

Sometimes Paloma giggled at her locker with the others and sometimes, when she wasn't quiet and tragic, thinking of a dead or missing parent perhaps, or even reliving the story of a not-quite-broken people still awaiting their champion, she was quiet and bright-eyed, *de pajarito*, a birdlike creature with something in her head beside a mouthful of *repeticiones* chorused by kids who were already locked up if they but knew it, prisoners of the present, captives of a half-dozen words.

What is Paloma thinking?

Sometimes she answered the teacher's questions and answered them well; and sometimes Tomás had the feeling that Paloma knew that someone behind her, someone who never spoke in class, had also found a use for his brain; someone was understanding each word of hers as it was spoken.

And once or twice she'd looked over her shoulder, her eyes moving just a little more quickly than her head to single him out. Perhaps when one of the teacher's questions floated on the air. Did she expect him to grin and nod with a *"sí, señora*, it is as my classmates say, some of us are as we are, we would starve without *caridad*, without *ayuda y asistencia*, without—how is it you say?—handouts. *Muchas gracias al gobierno.*" Another inclination of the head here.

Or was she waiting for him to stand up, not very tall, but standing, and say he had reason to believe the ranchers' attitudes were a little different when *la asistencia del estado* was for them?

Tomás sat in back where the rows of *estudiantes* seemed to get darker and more *macho*—*los chicos morenos* who sat behind the others—until you got to one boy even darker and quieter than Tomás, even more consumed by whatever glared overhead or howled within, one who was always looking at the floor and clenching and unclenching his fists. If his classmates had had to guess who would bring a gun to school one day, they would all have guessed that boy. Even Tomás would have guessed him. But he, whatever his name was, never brought a gun to school. Tomás did.

What is Paloma thinking? Does her head already hurt?

Yes, Tomás had brought it to school several times, his father's gun, carried it where it couldn't be seen, brought it again and again, the way in his dreams a mythic *bandido* rode up to and stared across the border night after night. Only Tomás knew the gun was there, and he had no more intention of suddenly standing up and firing at his classmates than of quietly ordering an incursion into the sovereign state of *Nuevo México* while he, Tomás, sat a tired yet eager horse, a horse only he could see beneath him, whose lathered flanks only he could feel.

❋ ❋ ❋

Perhaps as an old man gathering dust, when Tomás had lived more years than *el gran bandido* ever managed, he would accept the fact that he himself was not and would never be Pancho Villa. He would sit in the plaza if his border town had one by then and, if not, with his back against some wall, gathering *el polvo de los siglos* on his knees, on the backs of his hands, in his nostrils and in the corners of his eyes . . . until it was too hot to sit there any longer, or until he had read every dust-covered *palabra* in his *periódico*, whichever came first.

Then he would drag himself into the restaurant behind the gift shop, if either were still there, and order *la especialidad del día* . . . unless he was eating a somewhat different kind of meal in line with a similar bunch of aging *tipos*, losers every one, every one of them eating the same *mierda* off the same metal tray.

Perhaps he would still need only to close his eyes, and there would be plenty of time to do that, to see *el gran bandido* rising above himself, coming to understand that it was not what you could take from the rich that mattered: it was what you could get through to the poor, or they, with a manful assist, could get through to themselves.

Over and over again, Pancho Villa, behind his, Tomás's, closed lids, would realize this and then, once more, his battles lost to Obregon's superior battlefield techniques, fall from his realization, a blood-spattered figure, wrenching himself from history or oblivion—it hardly mattered—leading his surviving band over the *Sierra Madre* to a spot not that far from where the old man sat.

And the next day and the next he, Pancho Villa, would realize once again how foolish his forgetting had been, how *idiota* it was even to think of sending his ragged survivors raiding across the border, of an *incursión*; that he'd been right earlier thinking of

land, of schools, of low-cost loans to *los campesinos*; he'd wander
across the plaza to approach Tomás once again, from the side,
allowing his *armas* to jingle softly, his shadow to fall across the
news of a time he never lived to see, while waiting for an old man,
despite his resolution never to look up, to look up and see that *su
coronel, su general*, was not there, that a shadow without substance
had darkened his page . . . that the order for the raid would not be
cancelled after all . . . .

The raid that would give the *Graphic* of that long-gone day the
chance to editorialize on the natural laws governing the "expan-
sion of races," of the Anglo-Saxon in particular, over an "inferior
and unworthy race" meant to be displaced—if not now, later—by
one more "industrious, virtuous and war-like." And if the papers
advocating the settlement of *México* by the white race couldn't be
found in the library at middle school, they were right there in the
biblioteca pública.

❀ ❀ ❀

But Tomás was not riding with Pancho Villa, he was learning
English, and in class, perhaps *gracias a los años con su madre*, Tomás
always felt impatient with the others, the way he had to slow down
his own thoughts because the *anglos* seemed to think and speak one
word at a time rather than enjoy the flow of *palabras y sentimientos y
pensamientos* all coming together the way you breathe. It was even
possible with their one-word grunts that *yanquis* didn't think at all.
They knew nothing, that much was certain, not even their own history, and nothing, nothing at all, about his *México*, past or present.

He'd even heard a kid saying in the hall that spics were dark
because they were really *indios*—and the cowboys had known
how to deal with them. Here the kid raised an invisible gun to his
own head and pulled an invisible trigger. And the kid had spoken
quietly, sagely, through unmoving lips, leaning back against the
lockers like Billy the Kid, without the faintest idea that he had a
nearly terminal case of peer poisoning himself, that he didn't know
many more words of English than Tomás did.

Let the prisoners of the present talk about what they could
click to on their *computadoras domésticas* with restless fingers and
dancing feet. Let them add dot/coms to their speech. If you
wanted to find something really interesting, Tomás knew, you sat

still, you found a book of history or biography in the *biblioteca*, one that nobody had taken out for twenty years, and then, from time to time, you looked up from it, you stared through the window at a landscape that hadn't changed in eighty-five years if ever, in human terms, and thought your thoughts.

How he wanted to share those thoughts, how he wanted to open his jacket and show a book that, it seemed, if you looked at the dates inside the cover, no one else had read in all the years he had lived so far. It was even possible that he himself had been seen, by someone, the book open on the table before him, his eyes smoldering with accomplishments that it might not be given more than once to a man to achieve.

Of his own future, even then he didn't know why, he could not think.

But what is Paloma thinking? Of revoluciones, *of people straggling across the map behind her? Is she sad?* ¿Desanimada? ¿Desconsolada? ¿Por qué? ¿Por qué?

Paloma *had* noticed him first, he knew that now. Because he could still picture her looking over her shoulder at him, and to think it had been done in such a way that no one else ever noticed and even he couldn't see it clearly until now, in memory, when it was already too late.

❊ ❊ ❊

The fact is that Tomás, the boy of twelve, first saw Paloma, or the back of the head he was destined to explode, in English class where, he liked to believe, they both bowed before another language as rich, as deserving of respect, as their own. She did not arrive as romantically as he in a dusted bus grinding up from *la frontera*; but, he inferred, since she was always there before him, she had descended from another bus that picked children up off the ranches on the rural routes or she had walked with her girlfriends or had been carpooled by mothers. Paloma was born in the land of plenty, but Tomás was one of those who came in the back door, who could claim citizenship on the basis of *uno de sus padres*, living or dead, and was bused north every day to school.

North. After the twin border towns, in one of which an old man sat watching life and, for the moment, death pass him by; after the lines of *gringos* and *mexicanos*, the *menonitos* waiting with their old-fashioned wives, all face to face with *los procesos burocráticos* before they could drive their fancy *carros* or limping *cacharros*, for whatever reason, south into *México*; yes, every weekday, after *las escenas eternas de la frontera*, Tomás, heading north, knew the open spaces and the white dust *de la tierra de nadie* between two countries, the unchanged landscape.

He knew *la alba* in the winter as a dust-laden sun rose behind *las Floridas* and one boy anyway stared into a landscape large enough to hold all the tragedies of this world. On holidays, playing in the dirt streets because his pueblo had no plaza, he had known the tight swirling eddies, *los remolinos de polvo*, spinning in the heat, some no bigger than a man, than a boy. And he liked the English name for them, "dust devils."

He wondered if his mother was a dust devil now, if all the dead and missing were, for he had heard the truth in church "*polvos eres y en polvo te convertirás*," and sometimes a dust devil not much bigger than he was did follow him down the street and around the corner.

He had to run then, because if you got caught, as did happen, *el remolino* certainly wanted in, rushing at your eyes and ears as if it would be quite happy, *completamente en casa*, in your blood, in your veins, making you see as it saw, go where it spun you, perhaps allowing you to shake your head a little later the better to realize you had done exactly what it had wanted you to do all along. And what could he expect, growing up in a house with only one parent, with a mother missing before he was old enough to grunt perfect American and a father who was no cowboy?

But Tomás was learning English. He already had his favorites among the sayings, *los dichos como uno por morder el polvo*: "bite the dust." He liked the final sound of that, the feel of it on his lips and teeth like grit carried by the wind. He could picture a man who had been shot, suddenly on his face in the fine flat dirt that passed for a street, his mouth working without his even wanting it to, eating *tortillas de la tierra*, if there are such things, even as he gagged on the powdery earth itself and "croaked," which said it all. But what was "eat your heart out"? Probably something different from bite the dust. And to "bushwack" was to put someone to bed with a shovel. He liked that.

Tomás, the boy of twelve, didn't like movies about big city crimes, only *las películas de vaqueros*, the old ones that played on television again and again, especially ones with, for some reason, perhaps because he seemed such a gentleman, Randolph Scott. At the end of a Western so many men were dead they might as well have blown away, gone in *una tormenta de polvo*.

But no one ever shot *la heroína*, except by mistake. She was usually there at the end watching you ride up—all that killing business out of the way, behind you—waiting to open her arms to you. To be held by the heroine at the end was the dream that let Tomás fall asleep at night, even if a dream of *el bandido* riding with his men, shadowing the herd he was going to rustle to the border, leaving the weaker cows to the hungry along the way, or *el general,* the same man later, ordering Creel's cattle to be butchered at cost, or less than cost, for the poor in the streets of Chihuahua, might wake him up.

※　※　※

And yet there were those days when Tomás wasn't sure he wasn't an old man sitting in a relatively new plaza, one who had read and reread in his *periódico* the story of *el crimen patético*, and remembered looking at a boy who was looking back at him, a boy heading north from the border on a bus; a boy, apparently, with no one to talk to and with eyes as wide as the undone, the unlived . . . .

What is Paloma thinking? It must be something.

There were also days when he wasn't sure he wasn't the boy himself, one not that likely ever to exchange a word with an old man seated on a new bench or against an old wall, especially if the old man were himself.

But if there are points in time, and if this were one of them, *el incidente, el evento* itself—that which had occurred and been duly recorded, then the effort to comprehend seemed inevitably to arrive at this other, somewhat earlier point in return, one where man and boy gaze through the dusted glass of a straining school bus and one, or both, old man and boy, link one event to the other in the certainty that, without *el evento*, neither of them would ever amount to, or had ever amounted to, anything; they could be sure only of one *hecho*, one previously recorded fact: that one man destined to rise above himself, one man who just happened to have been born in 1878 and traversed this very spot where, at the end of another century, man and boy passed each other without a word, had traversed it several times himself—at least once in 1916—and had somehow, this man who at some point must have known his own future, spoken to them both.

As, once upon a time, which was another way of saying in 1894, it, Pancho's story, told it, *el hacendado*, the landlord *don Agustín López Negrete*, had insulted Pancho's twelve-year-old sister, Martina, and Doroteo, which was Pancho's real name—and Pancho wasn't really a lot older than his sister—had tried to kill the man, wounding him twice. Ever after he was an outlaw, the Napoleon from nowhere, the great-man-to-be from *San Juan del Río*, origins even humbler than the *pueblo fronterizo* Tomás had found for himself, a spot for some reason designated as *General R.M. Quevedo* on the maps of *México*.

Yes, Pancho's story was part of the boy's story, the story of Tomás, the boy soon, so soon, to know his future. The old man had his own story, of course, one that would not be worded by the lines of his face, one he would never tell to anyone now, not even to the boy, were he to visit him, because it wasn't necessary to tell it, it was enough to know it, parts of it, the parts that remained.

The old man had also worked his way north, from job to job, perhaps like *el bandido*, perhaps not. He did not remember nearly killing himself for practically nothing in the mines, or killing cowboys to rustle a herd of rich man's cattle. He did remember one moonless night on a north-south trail, trailing a string of unbroke and green-broke horses toward the border when he himself was only a boy. He remembered when visibility in the ravines fell to absolute zero and you could hear the trail crumbling as you passed and the older men on either end of the bunching animals sang to the horses and the horses went on placing unseen foot in front of unseen foot, and he himself, the boy, was somewhere in the middle and perhaps—and if it wasn't true then it was now—the cowboys sang to him too.

❀ ❀ ❀

Tomás knew that if history ever came his way, it was unlikely to arrive in the sad form of a fallen and forgetful Pancho Villa, come to shoot up the place once more, or even just to scout it out, *de incógnito*, slouching not quite disguised through a border town that is even more defenseless now than then because the nature of warfare had changed unrecognizably, spying his way through the decades, the centuries, for the time had never been ripe for a cross-border raid *a caballo*.

It was even possible that the invasion of the U.S. on horse-back had never meant anything and, if *el general* had known it then, he had certainly not forgotten it now. Even to his absurdly overarmed *fantasma*, perhaps even to the few tourists, who did not linger long, there was nothing of romance or color in the flat buildings not that far from the border . . . certainly not when you counted the young American defenders who shouldn't have had to die so young in a century in which so much was yet to happen, so much was yet to be asked of them, and you counted the not-so-young *mexicanos* who didn't deserve to die achieving nothing at all.

And perhaps when he was sufficiently ancient, and sufficiently defeated, to accept the fact that he, Tomás, had not himself shed tears on the news of Madera's death or won the battle of Zacatecas, or seen his victories come to nothing in the days that followed, he would see how meaningless it too, *el evento*, had been that one day in the next to last month of the last year of the so recently past century, a boy of twelve had crossed the border *con muchas fuerzas*, if not *violencia*, in his heart, crossed as he had every *día de semana* for as long as he could remember.

The boy had ridden a school bus north, as always, a big yellow bus roaring feebly every weekday on the way to, or from, a school that accepted all kinds, providing they could prove at least one parent was a *ciudadano* or a *ciudadana* of the good ol' U.S. of A., only this time with one side of his jacket heavy and leaning against his heart.

And the old man would go back and tell himself the story, not of Pancho Villa, sole invader of these United States, at least at this point in space (a little east, or west, of nowhere), for though Villa had, undoubtedly, been the boy's hero too, his story was known; no, the old man would go back and tell himself the story of the boy, the boy himself. Then perhaps he could claim that he understood *el crimen patético del niño*, if not *la incursión lastimosa* of Pancho Villa.

And so, of an afternoon, as the heat gathered and the dust of one century settled upon that of another, the old man would begin again the story of the boy. Not that anyone would ever want to hear his *versión*, not when they had the four-line narrative to stick in their ears, the *redundancias* squeezed between *repeticiones* of *sim-*

plificaciones, between eye-jarring *anuncios* and ear-splitting *cacofonía* on their *televisors*. Yes, he would ask himself, before it got too hot to think, just what the boy had in mind.

Whatever had he had in mind? Loitering in the hall near a locker he never passed without longing? Stopping a lovely girl with whom he had never spoken? Opening his jacket to reveal a gun he had never intended to show to anyone and certainly not to her? And she? What was she supposed to do? Were her eyes to fill as she raised her arms to him *como la heroína* at the end of a Western? Right there in the hall as the herd thundered past?

"Oh Tomás, I never realized your head hung so heavy under the pitiless glare from above, that the whirlwind within was so near to wrenching you apart, that you could not even once more grin and look down and swallow *los denigraciones* of the *anglos* like the dust in the back of your throat."

Or was that just a bad translation of her never-to-be-spoken lines? Perhaps, eyes averted not to draw the attention of *la masa*, of those who wouldn't understand, she'd speak to him in Spanish, more quietly, as was her fashion, and more to the point.

"*Mira, Tomás, la vi, tu pistola. La esconde ahora, la trae a tu casa, no la traigas aquí de nuevo. Hablamos mañana, tú y yo, sin tu pistola. Hablamos de tus pensamientos y de los libros que tú has leído. De Pancho Villa si tú quieres.*"

And she'd be gone, until tomorrow, with nothing having happened, no harm done, no life ruined in a second, not even hers.

But perhaps, he wonders, an old man wonders, if he is looking at the story a little too near the end. What about the afternoons and evenings leading up to *el evento, el incidente*? What about weekends, the days alone? For in spite of, or perhaps because of, the fact that you only get so many, an old man can't help knowing that one day does indeed lead to another. Just as one story leads to another and sometimes you don't even know which one you're following, which one you're telling yourself.

And so, once upon a time, that is on Saturdays and Sundays, Tomás always thought of her. And sometimes he just sat and watched the birds, as if he were already old. There weren't that many birds in his *pueblo fronterizo*, maybe it was too dry, and the few doves always appeared in pairs, though you did sometimes see one alone, lost, unpartnered, *sin pareja, sin parejo*, round eyes wide, seeking the mate never to be known or the mate lost in a moment . . . .

But what about the thing itself, ordained or not, predictable or not, avoidable or not? What about the event? No, it is too vivid, too present. To be postponed as long as possible, no matter how the tale is told, to whom or in what version. *Sin embargo . . . .*

It was after lunch, the halls crowded, filled with the squeak of identical footwear and rather similar minds, that Tomás had stepped close to Paloma. He was just going to open his coat and show her the gun, as if he were inviting her to share his thoughts *más recóndito*, his dusty landscapes and his books, as a preface to inviting her to walk around the tiny park on the American side of the border, meeting her halfway some day when he didn't have to take the bus all the way to school.

That night, perhaps he'd take her home, on his side of the border, if his father weren't there, to see *una película de vaqueros* with Randolph Scott, though he wasn't at all sure she would agree to come or would be as enthusiastic as he was about Westerns. But it was better than showing up in a ten-gallon hat smelling of imaginary horses, so all could see that, even today, even for one so young, or so old, it was possible to be something of an historian with both boots in a time that, no matter how hard you tried to make it, would never, never come again. It would be better than speaking his piece too *rápidamente* between the ratchety clang of her locker and the click of a classroom he didn't share with her. Between lives.

"*Mira*, Paloma, I am not like the others, you must listen to me, you must meet my horse, we will go riding together on *mi caballo*, bareback, high in *las Floridas*, we will look down on your town and mine, on the border between us . . . ."

Though maybe he had just planned to shoot the words out of his mouth before he could be known for a fool, as if he would fire them all off in a breath/or two/or three:

"*. . . yoteamoPaloma/yotequiero/nomeolvides. . .*"

But Tomás had shot the heroine; not *los malos*, the dumbed-down crowd; only her. It was not supposed to happen that way, not in a Western. The bad guys were supposed to have blown away, but he stood in the hall, looking down at a ruined girl, the gun heavy in his hand and the kids who, after all, were not quite as *estupidez* as he, falling back and then, one of them, he supposed, stepping forward to remove the gun from his hand. He had been taken into custody. His horse was nowhere near, not even in the parking lot. He had not galloped off to the south through the gap in the fence he had cut the night before. He had sat in the back of the squad car, a kid himself, for once somehow at one with kids who only stood and stared. And the cop looking at him in the rear-view mirror must have seen this as he spoke to the boy's reflection.

"You'd just better hope she doesn't die, kid."

That seemed to have been said to him again and again, though maybe only once, and she did. She died the next day, barely having survived his touch to the back of her neck twenty-four hours. She died, though it might have been simpler if he had.

Alive, living, she would have gone on to become whatever she was to become. Yes, she would have forgotten him, her first friend of the mind, of the spirit, but it wouldn't matter because she was going on, she was going to do whatever she was going to do anyway. She would rise, and he was never going any further than the plaza, which wasn't built yet, in which he would sit and read, waiting forever for the shadow of *el gran bandido* to fall across the very last dust-covered word in his *periódico*, the shadow of the Robin Hood of *San Juan del Río* who had already come and gone eighty-five years ago.

What is Paloma thinking? Maybe he has the answer now. Why, yes, it's nothing. Nothing at all.

But Paloma was rising, rising on wings of misunderstanding, on the sweet breath of love, rising high over middle school, over the town and the highway to the south, over the border with its twin nowhere towns, places no one would stop if there were not a fence between them and men in uniform watching and waiting for you. She was not watching him beneath her, lost in a landscape that was still white but would soon be black. And in twenty-four hours of pain, which was all he had ever given her, there would not be time for a single thought of him, not one, though if there had been, it would have been forgiving, he was sure, simply because he could never forgive himself and knew she knew it.

It was the last thing she could do on this earth.

And this even if she had not actually seen him at the moment, even if she did not know, if she had only mind enough left to wonder, who it was, who had done it.

But for him, still alive, not a day would pass, as they say in the newspapers, that he wouldn't think of it, of what he'd done, that he didn't wonder why he'd done it and not something else, put the gun to his own head, *por ejemplo*, and erased the history that would never be written anyway.

Torn the book. Apart.

No, he knew that now, not a day would pass.

But Paloma was still rising, rising far overhead, *una ave de paso fue en una tormenta de polvo*, of confusion, of bewilderment, of blood and the smell of gunpowder, and he was, *al instante*, not a boy with a gun but an old man with a newspaper, a dreamer of times past who had never even spoken to the boy.

Though perhaps there was a boy on the bus just passing, another or the same, looking out, looking right through an old man where he sat on his bench, already invisible, one foot in hell; just like one of his own feet if he, the boy, but knew it. There he was now: boy or bird flying into darkness, a darkness where he would probably not be together with his beloved, but a different darkness altogether, yet one not absolutely different from the intolerable glare, the brightness where a dove sits immobile, dazed by the sun, beak open, alone, waiting.

Nick Carter, oil on paper

Road Work in Baja and the Middle School Boy

He turns warning posts on their sides and makes
orange hurdles, bright as carrots, set crosswise
into the ditch like ladder rungs down the center
of Calle Guanabana. He tests for firmness,
kicks one end and then the other, before placing
the next and the next, as if planting hazards
for futures, maybe entrance exams for universities, or
a señorita's refusal to dance. Twice, he's run at them,
left the ground, soared with legs stretching
a high, long stride, as if in a moon race
where gravity holds no one back. Then, perhaps
desire outreaches pace, or ground becomes a draw
not to be ignored, and he is galloping the channel
left by earlier laborers, feet touching this world
step by step.

Dia de Los Muertos Conversations

There are the marigolds bunched to earth with flounces *de amarillos*, castanets on their sepals, dust *naranja* on the garden fingers where little bones *baille* on headstones and sugar teeth are *azul*. There are the *sombreros negros* laced with silver, pumpkin seed pearls bleached *blancas*, cinnamon and *manzanas rojas*. There are the little bones turned of dust, noon or sunset, *la noche y la mañana*, little bones turned of dust. They become the trickle that feeds stones and sheep with song. When they laugh, the wind sighs and silences, sighs and silences like bells hung on a new moon when *la bruja's* skirts flash past.

The Lady of the Dead is dust and whispers to dust, telling the little bones who sit with marigolds blossoming from their chests. She loves the sighs and silences between fists and bowls of grain, how the grain plays *armónica*, *y el perro* thumps *la pandereta*, and all the little bones dance.

When did marigolds learn flamenco? When did they don castanets? When did I hear the little bones singing on their way to dust? The child girl with ears as long as a truck has climbed up the ribs of the woman to hear what she heard at one. And a smaller child, who nests inside, has climbed up the ladder of neck to hear the bells toll on.

I will hear them talking, one speck of bone to the next, and the next, and then they will turn to me, me with my *azul* teeth, me with my marigold skirts *y camisas rojas*, me with blossoms *amarillos* floating over this *cabeza del azúcar* where *loco* thoughts once curled, and we will dance, the way little bones dance, until we are singing water, dew on the bells of the moon.

Peregrinaje sin fin / Never Ending Journey

Were you perhaps a butterfly
in the temples of Tikal and Monte Albán?
Or the afternoon silence
when just a sliver of light remained
on the horizon?
Maybe you were a guinea pig
on a patio in Machu Picchu, waiting your turn
to quell the gods' hunger with your blood . . . .

And what was it like when you
and the sun virgins
wove royal clothes for gods and lords
and blankets to cover mummies in their tombs?

You helped draw the Nazca Lines
from which you inherited your nomadic ways
and your round proportions.

Now, on the edge of the harshest millennium
you search the records of memory
and the blood coursing through your veins
confirms that you were part of that world
burnishing the friezes of Chan Chan
and toiling as an astrologer in Copán.

You watched artisans design realistic pots
and ancient cubists polish Coaticlue.

A Hindu in Haridwar's temples,
a Bedouin in the endless desert
you traveled from pointed pyramids
to shortened pyramids.

In the archeological site San Agustín
you shook the *maguey* plants
to extract their secret
and nourished yourself with fresh *pulque* . . . .

Within your wanderer's soul
is a piece of eternity
from times long ago
that does not stop this march toward the unknown.

Translated from the Spanish by Maureen Contreni

Alice Lindsay Price, pencil, copyright 2001

A La Fuerza / By Pure Force

Now, at the ripe old age of seventy-three, I finally understand that my father was wrong when he said, "Nothing ever fits by pure force, *m'hija*. Not even old shoes." So he warned me when I was a child, lulling me to sleep in the hammock, under the flamboyant tree, at dusk. Tired after another day hacking at sugarcane—that ungrateful bush that crushed his spirit, broke his back and his dreams—for a fistful of beans. There, swinging in the hammock, he counseled me, at the hour when the mosquitoes hold sway.

Today, I still hear his rasping voice, hardened by too much liquor and tobacco—neither of which, in the end, managed to assuage his sadness. "Not even shoes fit by pure force, *m'hija*," he would murmur, and I, that little girl nodding off in his arms, believed him.

I believed him until I was thirteen, until that dreadful day that he took me to the city and delivered me to the rich people. After all, it was time for me to earn a living, and furthermore, "Here, you will want for nothing, *m'hija*, take good advantage of what these people give you; remember, not even shoes . . . ."

"Will fit by pure force." I finished the old saying, because his voice caught in his throat and tears flooded his eyes. I promised to do my best in this new life, though I had never needed anything other than his scent of woodsmoke and wet earth.

As it happened, in the rich people's house, everything did fit. It all came in by pure force. The *señora*'s screams pierced me, for not picking over the lentils well enough, for failing to get all the stains out of the soiled underwear, for washing the dishes poorly, for speaking like an Indian peasant. The slaps crossed the threshold from all directions, especially from the cook, for getting in her way in the kitchen, for messing up the pantry, for poking my nose around and spying on her when she was necking with the gardener. The pinches from the spoiled girls also came in, unbridled, for not having made up the beds, not having braided their hair perfectly, or simply because they were bored and had nothing else to do.

The *patrón* entered my room one day, without knocking. He came in drunk and vehement, to teach me that by pure force, everything could enter—of course it could! With just a shove and a smack or two. By pure force, *the shoe will fit*. By pure force, even

Cinderella's glass slipper fits the callused foot of a sleazy Indian like me. No point in being stubborn. Better to close one's eyes and go limp. Better to let *everything* go limp—most of all, one's conscience.

I wanted to show my father his mistake. I returned barefoot, walked all the way to my village, but I arrived too late. In the hammock, in the shade of the flamboyant, I waited for him until dusk fell. I waited for him all that night and many more. I waited until all the nights fell, at once, on my broken body. When the cane-burning began, I ran over the cloak of ashes, ferreting through desert rubble. I overturned rocks, scratching at fire scars and clearing away scorched roots, without finding him. The dusty rumor that clung to my footprints swore to have just seen him, dead in some ravine. *The cane—and the drink—took him away*, it whispered. *He was taken kicking and screaming*. By pure force.

I set out again headed North, barefoot, walking on my charred soles, chasing that fistful of beans that had so eluded my father. I crossed mountains, rivers and borders, doggedly pushing ahead, my punctured body my only shield—the same shield that so deftly deflected misfortune and mishap. And so I arrived here, intact, on the other side. To lush, irrigated valleys. Abundant orchards. It was then that I, a pierced woman, demanded everything from life.

Yes it can, damn right it can, has been my motto. With my eyes closed and my conscience stifled—but lucid—I earned it all: my living, a roof over my head, a full pantry and a pile of children and grandchildren, whom I never gave away to anyone. I surrendered my life to the apple—that ungrateful fruit that has left my back bent but my dreams intact. And now, though these prison bars would detain me, my essence flees. Like sand through a sieve, my old age slips through the cracks. And I walk free, leisurely, through rich fields. I walk barefoot, a dark-skinned Cinderella, smelling of woodsmoke and wet earth, which I reclaim day by day, with this arthritic fist, by pure force.

Translated from the Spanish by Wendy Call

Semilla

A doña Francisca Rojas

Vengo del canto del colibrí
de la sangre olorosa de volcán
canta el arriero a su paso con las bestias

Las vías del tren
los días fríos de Tlaxcala
con los volcanes taciturnos e impecables

Soy un camino de oyameles
una gota de tiempo
un grito perdido en el maguey
un aliento de yegua en brama

Nostalgia de la lluvia
de las flores la estación
y las lágrimas del sauce

Seed

for Doña Francisca Rojas

I come from the hummingbird's song
from the volcano's sweet-smelling blood
the skinner sings as he drives his mules

Train tracks
cold days in Tlaxcala
with faultless, silent volcanoes

I'm a path of *oyamels*
a drop of time
a lost cry in the *maguey*
a breath of a mare in heat

Nostalgia for the rain
for the flowers the station
and the willow's tears

Translated from the Spanish by Toshiya Kamei

Túneles desiertos

Caminamos por túneles desiertos
en la espera del rostro oculto
$\qquad\qquad$ de la noche pétrea

Buscas mi voz y aliento metálico
bailas en el ombligo de una ciudad
$\qquad\qquad$ *surgida del agua*
donde el viento gime preso
$\qquad\qquad$ *bajo el Zócalo*

Somos un brote de espinas
$\qquad\qquad$ sobre las ruinas
$\qquad\qquad\qquad$ de la ciudad

Desert Tunnels

We walk through desert tunnels
waiting for the hidden face
     of the stone night

You look for my voice and metallic breath
you dance in the center of a city
      rising from the water
where the wind moans
     under the Zócalo

We're a shoot of thorns
    over the ruins
      of the city

Translated from the Spanish by Toshiya Kamei

Mexico's Waters Are Only for Newlyweds

No one welcomes our bodies in Puerto Vallarta.
They fear we witch its waters with marital failure.

An affair every even year of marriage and this is another
makeshift reconciliation—*mojitos* and a week of beach

you've charged to your credit card: penance
of the easiest order. Each morning, your footprints lead

from the beach to me where you move my body
against the grit we've shaken off in sleep. Sand everywhere,

we've given up on trying to stay clean. Nine years of marriage—
your lust's no longer monstrous, my sarong little

to hide. The wave-wet sand won't welcome us
the way it did the night you gave me your last name.

The sky was honey-mooned that night, its light golden
across your shoulders. Today is only sun-blast in our eyes

as we stare beachward toward newlyweds shimmering
like the wished-on dimes I've tossed in the hotel fountain.

Sierra Madre del Sur

—after Leopardi's "L'Infinito"

When I am blind, at last,
to ego, my thoughts ascend
beyond the hedges, past
this lonely hill I love.

It's then I know the Earth,
how soon we'll be uncoupled.
The thought upends me, leaves
my Earthen heart toppled

in silence such as the dead
must hear. I fear Heaven
only less than the Hell
I imagine: this mountain

chiseled to rubble, condos
along its back, birdsong
like the whiskey tenor
of the logger-saw. Nightlong

I'll dream but disinvite
eternity, forgo
the blessed pall of light,
the treeless world beyond.

It Matters

that the *casa* rises,
orange as the dawn sky
under cloud and blue,

impatiens—white, red, pink—
spilling from terracotta pots
along the balustrade;

that feathery jacaranda leaves flutter
and the bells of La Parrochia wake us
at six a.m. each morning;

that the gnarled woman begging
on the street was once young and agile
and that someone give her

a few pesos when she reaches out
from the sidewalk by the bank
in the sticky heat of late afternoon;

that even here I remember
my father's laugh and the weight
of my mother's disappointments,

while *les étoiles*, *las estrellas*, the stars
burn through the sky's dark cloth
no matter what I call them;

that prickly pear cacti are delicious
although the Big Bang defies
common sense and intuition,

and earth and sea offer their riches
freely to the boy playing
with a stick outside La Casa Rosada;

that he never have to hold a gun
and the bells always reach his ears,
pulsing through clear morning air.

Last of the Ballerina I Was

Her gaze swept along her arms,

the way I imagine a tree
must follow from its center to see the world,

& she pulled herself from each
spot of the stage, as if it were bliss

there, but she wanted

something else, unnamable to me now
as the thoughts
                of a starry animal,

music pleading *wait*,
& *stay* —

      I can still hear
the violins, & feel her last jeté,

how the stage rippled beneath her
as dusk ripples in the slipstream

of a bird

        whose sudden ascension

strands its shadow on the shore.

Alice Lindsay Price, pencil, copyright 2001

Directing the Happy Times

Think April, late, when all things tilt, quiver
with color and rain. Begin hibiscus, drip

like a woman in wet clothes. With deeper curve
magnolia, you ache and brown. Last drop

knock down the honeybee; on three, it bobs,
a cork in water, that's its time to shine.

Wisteria, study the air where it throbs.
Be amethyst. Focus. I'll need the vine

to fully engage the tree, lilies to white
one by one as Mother walks the lane.

It must be this precise or, simply put,
she'll get distracted, fail to read her line.

She will not laugh, the waiting stagehands' cue:
(lights down) Enter the shadows who carry you.

*After its acceptance by *Nimrod*, "Directing the Happy Times" was selected by Mark Strand to appear in *Best New Poets 2008*.

Silence is a Mother Tongue

Large birds push off from branches, heads down,
their soggy wings turning like oars. Beneath a net
    of mosquitoes, a corner of the lake's filmy surface
has thickened to a palette of lime, brown, and milky-blue.
    When she was well my mother gardened—plush
black irises, heavy orchids. What I have left
    are the sustained gazes between us. By the playground,
a fish-shaped kite, snagged on a power line, sways.
    His clear fins shimmer. I remember the summer
I overturned a dingy rock in the garden and found, like teeth
    grown in quiet, a cluster of quartz crystal. I showed my mother
in the kitchen. Blackbirds walked the clothesline;
    their pencil-yellow beaks etched the stillness. Our silences
were like this, something turned over, her eyes assessing it.

Manly Johnson, photograph

Brothers

I went to see Abuela on my way home from school. I had a plastic bag in my hand, filled with oranges that stretched the handle so much it was beginning to cut my palm. I rested the bag on the floor of the elevator while I waited for it to take me up to Abuela on the tenth floor. I shook my palm out, a line of red spots forming across it like a trail of ants. The elevator doors opened on the fourth floor and two tall, lanky bodies entered, their gangly arms flailing, gliding, tan and bony, under worn cotton t-shirts. They both wore faded jeans and I could see they were brothers, though one had a scar on his forehead that made him look older. He was a few inches taller than the other, and his hair, dark and wavy, hung a few inches longer.

Two sets of black eyes landed on me, critical and curious, like a doctor seeing a new patient. They leaned against the opposite side of the elevator like slinky giants, almost feminine in the way their hips turned crooked, like a model's, their thin waists becoming apparent under their clothing.

A pair of oranges rolled out of my plastic bag and across the elevator floor to their feet. Neither moved to pick up the fruits and I crouched down to reach for them, my hand reaching between their sneakers while they lowered their heads to watch me move about the floor. When the doors opened on the tenth floor, I turned to them, trying to give a polite smile, but I knew my face must have come across as fearful. Their black stares suddenly seemed amplified, and their lips curled upward into a strange smile.

"We're going to the roof," the taller one said. His voice was deep, sounding much older than his face appeared. "Come find us up there if you want."

The elevator doors closed between us before I could answer, dividing us like a stage curtain. I turned around and walked down the hall to my grandmother's apartment. She'd left the door unlocked for me and I went straight into the kitchen, setting the oranges in a bowl on the breakfast table. I found her in her bedroom, reading the Bible in a chair that used to be used only by my grandfather.

"I feel him when I sit here," she said, closing her eyes as she reached for me.

We hugged and I was careful not to hold her too tightly. My mother always warned me about my Abuela's weak bones before I came for a visit. Hug her too tightly and she might break.

Her wine-colored hair glowed in the dim light. The sun burned on the horizon outside but she always kept the blinds drawn, only letting in cracks of light because too much of it hurt her eyes. A sliver of light landed directly across the pages of her Bible, and she skipped the paragraphs that remained in the shadows.

"Jesus' temptation in the desert," she hummed, "Forty days with no food, and the devil taunting him with logic." I nodded as she spoke, my eyes wandering to the wedding picture of my grandparents hanging on the wall behind her. Abuelo looked happy, as I'd never seen him. He'd been bitter during my entire lifetime. Abuela looked thrilled, even surprised to be posing for her own wedding picture. She once told me she couldn't believe a man could love her so much.

"*No hay nada peor que la razon.* Logic is the enemy, Bianca, remember that. Truth is separate from reason."

I nodded. She closed her Bible and we talked about the neighbors who made too much noise, about my mother and how hard she had to work painting fingernails since Papi had left her.

"Shameless," Abuela said, referring to my father.

Her face scrunched as if she'd just eaten a sour fruit. "To abandon you both and leave you with nothing."

I nodded and told her I had to leave. I didn't like to take the bus back home when it was late. I was mugged once on the bus, and sitting in the plastic seats, enduring the ride home, through decrepit areas, was an hour of torture.

"Prepare yourself, darling, I'm going to die soon."

She said the same thing every time we parted ways and I learned to overlook it, a minor detail in our little ritual.

"You're going to outlive all of us, Abuela," I told her and kissed her on the top of her head.

As I waited for the elevator, I thought about the two boys I'd seen earlier. They'd said they were going on the roof. I'd never been up there. I felt a pulling in my chest as I stepped into the elevator and my arm seemed to command itself to extend to the top-floor button and press it hard. I stepped out, walked down the corridor to the emergency stairs, climbed them and pushed the escape door open. I crept onto the cement stage of the roof of the building and saw the silhouettes in the distance, as if across a field.

They saw me and I heard a whistle. The shorter one pushed his dark, oily mane off his face and handed me a cigarette when I stood in front of them.

"Don't tell me your name," he said, "I want to name you myself."

His voice was infantile, scratchy with a tinge of falsetto.

I took the cigarette, unsure what to do with it. I'd never smoked before.

"What will you name her?" asked the older one. I couldn't tell if they were serious or mocking me, but I stood there, waiting for my name to be given to me.

"Pigeon," said the younger one. "That's what you are. Like a dirty little street dove. I'm naming you Pigeon."

"What are your names?"

"Taro," said the older one.

"Blaise," said the younger one.

The sun had already set and I knew that my bus ride home would be very uncomfortable. I would spend the hour clutching my purse in my lap, avoiding the eyes of each stranger who boarded, sitting up front near the driver so that the security camera would be pointed at me though I'd heard those things didn't actually work. My stomach turned at the thought, yet I couldn't pull myself away from the two thin bodies on the roof.

"Are you brothers?" I asked them. My voice sounded so juvenile. I hated it.

They nodded, then Taro said, "What happened to your oranges?"

"I brought them to my grandmother. She lives on the tenth floor."

"Will you bring us oranges next time you come?"

I nodded.

"Come tomorrow. We'll wait for you."

✿　✿　✿

My heart floated still in my chest as I waited to arrive home that night. The bus rolled along the avenues slowly. My breaths were short and thin. I closed my eyes hoping that when I opened them I would be at the bus stop by my house. I closed and opened them dozens of times before I arrived. My mother was already asleep. I watched her from the doorway of her bedroom for a few moments. She looked so tired. She could sleep for days and it would never be enough to make up for how much my father's departure had exhausted her.

❖　❖　❖

The next day, I bought six oranges for the brothers. I stepped out of the elevator on the fourth floor, not knowing which door to knock on. I stood in the middle of the corridor for several minutes, hoping for a sound, or even an odor to lead me to one door instead of another. Then a door creaked open and Blaise's body emerged from the doorway.

"Pigeon," he said, and waved me over.

I handed him the oranges and he pulled me inside by my elbow. The apartment was just like my grandmother's in shape, one large bedroom and one large living room, with a kitchen off to the side. Yet while my grandmother's apartment was filled with furniture, rugs, collectibles, framed photos, and other objects that marked her lifetime, the brothers' apartment was white, from floor to ceiling, with one sofa pulled open into a bed, and two inflatable chairs. The door to the bedroom was shut and the kitchen didn't have more than appliances in it. Taro was spread across the sofa-bed, wearing no shirt and only a pair of scissor-cut green shorts.

He pushed himself up on his elbows when he saw me. Blaise took my hand in his and led me to the bed. I sat on the edge and he sat across from me in one of the plastic chairs.

"Now I have to kiss you," he said.

"Kiss me?"

"It's a proper thank you for the oranges, don't you think?"

I'd never been kissed before and I was partly terrified and partly excited at the prospect of having Blaise's greasy hair brush up against my cheeks and his fluffy pink and purple lips rush into mine the way I'd seen my father do to his girlfriend. He put his hand around the back of my neck and pulled me toward him, smashing our faces together. My eyes opened and closed nervously while my lips tried to find a place against his, but his mouth was too quick and moved feverishly so that I was lost and fell behind.

Blaise pulled away from me and the two brothers looked at each other.

"That was really terrible," Taro said. "How old are you, Pigeon?"

"Fourteen."

"Nobody ever taught you to kiss before?"

"No."

"Don't you have any brothers or sisters?"

"No," I said, though I wasn't really sure what that had to do with anything.

Taro looked thoughtful, even sympathetic. He pulled his body so that he was next to me on the edge of the bed and I felt his bare skin rub against my shoulder as he positioned himself. I thought he was going to kiss me but instead, he leaned forward and met his brother's face in the air between the three of us, and their lips arrived at one another's with precision. The top of Taro's mouth nibbled on Blaise's lower lip and their tongues reached for each other's, curving, turning, rubbing, and sucking, as their black lashes sealed shut over their eyes and they fell into a sort of trance before finally pulling apart. I realized I had not been breathing and began to choke.

"You bite too much," Taro told Blaise and then took my hand in his.

"It takes years of practice to kiss well, Pigeon. Don't feel bad."

I thought I would faint.

❊ ❊ ❊

I stayed with the brothers for another two hours. I didn't go to my grandmother's at all, and noticed the sky turn dark outside their windows, which had no curtains on them. I thought of the bus ride and Taro seemed to have read my mind.

"Don't worry," he said, "We'll drive you home."

❊ ❊ ❊

I looked forward to the end of the school day so that I could see Taro and Blaise. Sometimes they would come to pick me up at my high school, and I would crawl into the back seat while Taro slammed his foot on the gas and left a dust cloud behind us. He was reckless on the road, but I began to look for his smile, one that he reserved for rare moments of comfort, usually when I was talking to Blaise, never when the full attention was on him.

We went to a flea market in the center of the city. Crowds circulated, haggling for dingy artifacts and old clothing. Taro started running frantically, chasing an invisible chicken, and screaming as he pushed through the crowd, reaching for the ground as if the chicken were scurrying in between the legs of strangers. Blaise saw Taro's game and began playing too. The two of them ran as if they were chickens themselves, suddenly possessed, flapping their skinny arms like limp chicken wings and shrieking as if they were being chased by flying axes aiming for decapitation. The people of the flea market watched them in shock, while some laughed and others looked on in horror. Taro's tall body wriggled, and his eyes rolled back into his skull as he ran around in large circles. Blaise feigned the pecking motion of a chicken's head, flapped his imaginary wings and almost looked as if he were taking flight.

Taro passed me, pulled me onto his back, and we suddenly became a two-headed chicken, one chicken body mounted on the other, and he carried me through the crowd with the same airy speed, and I swung my arms in the air, flapping them like a wild chicken, screeching and cocking my head as the eyes of strangers glared at us.

When we were through, we slid onto the hood of the car, parked under a shady tree, and laughed until our kidneys vibrated against our spines. Taro put his arm around me and pulled me into his chest while Blaise played with the fingers of my right hand, pinching them like little pillows.

❊ ❊ ❊

Blaise was seventeen and Taro was eighteen. I met their father once, at their apartment, and he seemed incredibly young as well. He was taller than his sons, and just as thin, with massive hands. They told me he was a retired surgeon and I thought of my mother, who was about his age, and worked so hard at her low-paying job. Sometimes, I thought of my mother marrying Taro and Blaise's father, and what it would be like if they were my brothers. We would be able to spend all our time together. But I didn't look at Taro like a brother. Though I was getting to know him, every day, he felt new to me, as if I were meeting him for the first time in the elevator when my oranges spilled to his feet. I was uneasy, yet excited around him, and his dark, almost mean stare was addictive.

He laughed so rarely that I began to act like a sort of clown, all in an effort to hear his faint chuckle. I'd jab my fingers in his side and tickle him, feeling his hard muscles tighten. He'd fold over and laugh reluctantly, then slide away, into his comfortable reclined position.

Taro was always stretched out, as if his long body was too much for him to support by sitting erect or standing. Blaise was the more nervous of the two, always milling around the room, looking into things, getting Taro a drink if he asked for it, answering the phone when it rang. At their apartment, I liked to lie next to Taro, inching closer to him as he inched away. One day, as he lay half-nude on the sofa-bed, in his frayed shorts, he instructed me to take off my shirt. I did, and felt a chill over my peachy skin and bra, pale next to his body, the color of a desert.

"Now we're the same," he told me, and kissed the top of my head.

I suddenly thought of my grandmother, and how I often kissed her in the same way. I realized it had been more than a week since I'd gone to see her, even as I spent endless afternoons in the same apartment building with Taro and Blaise.

☼   ☼   ☼

Taro and Blaise came to pick me up at school with a bouquet of roses. I thought they were for me but when I looked to the flowers eagerly, Blaise pulled them close to him, as if to keep from tempting me.

"We're going to play a little game, Pigeon."

"What's the first round?" Taro asked his brother.

"A hand on the inner thigh."

They stopped the car at a park, and Blaise and I remained in the car while Taro pulled a stem from the bouquet and stepped out of the car and towards the promenade where several women walked by in flirty, wispy sundresses.

We watched as Taro walked slowly, his jeans clinging to his thin legs, his t-shirt pressing against his chest as he walked into the wind and towards a blonde girl in a blue dress. He handed her the rose, spoke to her, and within minutes the two were settled on a park bench side by side. Taro moved in closer to her and she responded by lifting up her chin, opening her shoulders as if to reveal more of her breasts and entice him. He moved his hand forward and onto her knee and Blaise began to laugh within the car walls.

Taro's hand slid up the girl's thigh and pushed over her flesh so that his fingers were now hidden within the folds of her leg, under the edge of her dress. Her lips parted hungrily. He pulled his hand away quickly and stood up as if he'd discovered a horrible secret between her thighs, leaving her startled as he walked away and back to the car. Blaise laughed, as if intoxicated.

Next, it was up to Blaise to entice a girl into kissing him on the lips without kissing her first. This didn't seem so difficult to me since he'd already managed the same once with me, but I felt angry and foolish as I watched the brothers prod each other, taking turns pulling stems from the bouquet that would arrive at the hands of unsuspecting girls, some who the boys even reported to have engagement rings on their fingers.

Blaise succeeded and then Taro took the order to kiss a girl's neck, return with a shred from her skirt, one of her earrings, and finally, having a girl allow him to kiss her naked breast in plain view of any passerby.

Blaise cackled with each staged bravado, and I slid further into the back seat of the car, watching the bouquet of roses grow thinner and thinner with each girl who passed through the park.

＊　＊　＊

Mami and I went to visit Abuela together on a Sunday after church. We brought oranges and mangos and the elevator ride felt unusually long as I clutched the plastic bags. On the fourth floor, the elevator doors opened and my two brothers entered. They saw my mother beside me and acted as if they didn't know me, not offering so much as the false smile of a stranger. My mother eyed them and I knew they were riding up to the roof, cigarettes in hand.

When my mother and I exited the elevator on the tenth floor and the doors shut behind us, she let out a sigh.

"I can't believe how those boys have grown," she said, as if suddenly becoming aware of her own age in relation to theirs.

"You know them?"

"They're the surgeon's boys. They're wild kids, especially after what happened to their mother."

"What happened?"

"She died on the operating table while the father was assisting at the surgery. People say he killed her."

* * *

Abuela was reading the Bible. She was usually too tired to leave her apartment and attend church, so she watched it on television, listened to it on the radio, or simply spent extra time on the gospels.

"Blessed are those who have not seen yet believe," she said when my mother and I approached her.

"You look tired." Abuela sighed when her eyes finally focused on my mother.

My mother was distracted and I knew her mind was still on the boys from the elevator. I felt suddenly removed from them after hearing what she'd said. I wished I hadn't heard that about their father. I wanted to believe he was as beautiful a man as they were, infallible despite their strangeness.

"Mother, do you remember the surgeon's boys? The ones who lost their mother a few years ago?"

My grandmother looked instantly perturbed, the way she did when she thought of my father.

"Those are bad boys," she said. "They say they rape girls."

I wanted to defend them, to say that Taro and Blaise had been with me countless times and had never so much as touched me other than the fiasco of the kissing lesson. I wanted to protect the brothers I felt I'd inherited, and Taro, especially, because I felt I was beginning to love him.

"How can you say that?" I found myself arguing.

My grandmother looked hurt that I was questioning her and closed her Bible.

"I thought you said it was evil to gossip," I challenged her.

My grandmother nodded, slightly humbled, then added, "The devil is not wise because he is the devil, but because he is old."

"What does that mean?"

"It means that I have seen many things and you should trust these eyes even though they are old and are not as sharp as they once were."

Before we left, my grandmother turned to me and said, "Prepare yourself, Bianca, I am going to die soon."

I kissed her on her hair but thought of Taro kissing me, and instead of answering her like I always did, I thought of the sound of my name, Bianca, and how I missed the boys calling me Pigeon.

❊ ❊ ❊

I lay next to Taro on the sofa-bed. Blaise sat on the cold tile floor trimming his toenails with a silver clipper and the sound, like a ticking clock, marked my racing thoughts as I watched Taro's chest rise and fall with his breath. I wanted to ask him questions but was afraid. Taro had only been gentle with me but his general silence made me nervous that one day he would decide that he didn't want me around anymore. I wasn't sure why they had decided to take me on as a friend. Both Taro and Blaise were disturbingly handsome, like aliens from a planet where only beauty ruled. I wondered why Taro didn't have a girlfriend and then convinced myself that he probably did, yet he kept me out of her sight because I was only a child, after all. Blaise revealed more. He would stare at women longingly and when they played the bouquet game, sometimes it seemed hard for him to pull away from each of the girls. But Taro was always waiting for the next round.

I sucked in my belly and nudged Taro's forearm.

"Taro, why don't you have a girlfriend?"

He didn't turn to look at me. He stared at the television on the floor across from the sofa bed.

"I don't need one," he answered.

Blaise looked up from his toes and the brothers exchanged glances. I watched them watch each other, as if there was some sort of secret code in the way they blinked their eyes at one another.

Their father came in with a woman, round-hipped and sculptural, with masses of red curls cascading down her back. She looked nervous when she entered and saw us in the living room.

The brothers looked at her, and she nodded hello and walked into the bedroom while their father followed. He hardly ever spoke to me, as if I was some sort of ornament that his sons insisted on keeping. I didn't understand why there was so much silence among the men, when at other times they seemed so oddly close.

Taro stood up suddenly and went into the bedroom too, closing the door tightly behind him.

"Let's go," Blaise said, standing up quickly and tossing me my sandals. They landed on the sofa bed beside me.

"Where?"

"Doesn't your mother wonder where you are every night?'

"She gets home late and then goes to sleep."

"It's not right. I'm going to take you home."

The next time I was with the brothers, I mustered up more courage. When Taro and I were lying on the bed next to each other, I touched him lightly and waited until he faced me and I had his full attention.

"Taro, will you teach me how to kiss?"

His face didn't change at all. He looked as if he'd expected those words, or as if I had said something else.

He leaned in and put his lips on mine and I thought I would devour him whole, but there was resistance in his lips. His mouth remained on me yet he lowered his chin so that his lower lip was pulled away, taunting me. I moved in closer, put my arms around his neck, and for a moment we were tightly pressed together but then he pushed me away and the distance between us on the sofa-bed seemed to grow by miles.

"What did I do wrong, Taro? Just teach me, I'll learn."

"You're a disaster, Pigeon. Just pay attention."

He looked to Blaise who then came over and sat down next to his brother. Their lips formed a fast path to one another and they began kissing with melodic vigor, each motion smooth and fluid, as if they'd rehearsed a thousand times before. I climbed off the bed while they were still kissing and put on my sandals.

Blaise pulled away from his brother first and turned to me, as I opened the door to leave the apartment. "You're supposed to watch and learn, Pigeon."

"Did anyone ever tell you guys that what you do is really weird?"

Somehow, I still felt like the fool in the room.

"Blaise has more patience than me," Taro sighed, "He'll teach you how to kiss. Come here."

I walked slowly back over to them and Blaise took my hand. He pulled me over to him and hugged me before lunging into my lips, sensing my gums and throat with his tongue. We continued for several minutes while Taro watched and I wished it were his mouth on me and not his brother's.

❊ ❊ ❊

"God hates the sin, not the sinner," my grandmother paraphrased the Bible, as she often did. She rarely remembered passages word for word, as many of her religious friends did. Rather, she'd make them her own and reiterate them in her plain language.

We sipped tea together in her kitchen, the bowl of fruits between us, toppling over with the new oranges I'd brought for her. I held her rosary in my hand. She'd just given it to me, another to add to the collection of a dozen that I already had at home. She was always giving me her rosaries, telling me they were a part of her body, falling away as she prepared for death. I rolled the beads of the rosary around in my fingers.

"I've been thinking of those boys since your mother reminded me of them. Those boys . . ." Abuela's voice faded and she gave herself the sign of the cross. "Their father forgave the unforgivable sin."

My eyelids ripped open.

"What do you mean?"

"He forgave, or perhaps he tried to take the sin for himself. You see, sin spreads like a virus, infecting a family for generations."

She looked suddenly exhausted and I wanted to prod her for more information but I didn't have the heart to make demands when she looked so bothered by her memory.

❊ ❊ ❊

When I returned home, I found my mother reading in her bed, her face creased with wrinkles of fatigue and her eyes marked with shadowy bags.

"What's the unforgivable sin?" I asked her, as I stood in her doorway.

I knew she was surprised at my question but she seemed to sense my urgency for knowing the answer.

"Everything is forgivable."

"When people talk about the unforgivable sin, what is it?"

"In the Bible, it says it's blaspheming the Holy Spirit."

I failed to see how it related to the brothers. I stood quietly, unsatisfied with the response.

"Abuela said that the boys, the tall ones, the surgeon's kids, that they committed an unforgivable sin. I want to know what they did."

My mother's face changed. She seemed suddenly younger, the way I remembered her when I was a child and would sit on her lap and cry into the folds of her blouse. She was Snow White to me, the most beautiful and pure creature that existed. Her eyes became round and soft, the way they were when she told me my father had left.

"It's a terrible story, Bianca. I don't want you to hear about such ugly things. Just keep away from those boys. They're not good people."

I couldn't tell her how entangled with them I'd already become.

"I already know that they say that the father killed the mother while she was in surgery."

"They say he let her die. They could never prove it was murder. They say that he did it so that she would never tell what the son had done."

"Which of the sons?"

"The older one."

I thought of Taro, petrified to hear more.

"I saw their mother a few times. She was a beautiful woman, but very broken-looking. She always looked ashamed. They say that she tried to leave her family many times, that she told people her boys were sick."

My mother paused, uncomfortable with what she was about to say.

"They say the older son raped his mother."

❃ ❃ ❃

The only way that I could live with what I had learned was by not believing it. My mind turned the tale of the vicious son and victimized mother into a work of fiction and I dismissed it, returning to the brothers' lair, pressing even closer to Taro when I lay next to his bare body on the sofa-bed. I convinced myself that it was impossible for him to be a predator. I thought of him as a savage angel, rough in his gestures yet still holy. It was jealousy, and not justice, that finally moved me to ask questions.

Their father came home with a woman, one I had seen before, on the trail that led from the entrance of the apartment to the father's bedroom. She settled in, but after an hour, the father left the apartment. When he had been gone a few minutes, her voice called to Taro from the bedroom. He stood up quickly, as if in reflex, and disappeared into the bedroom. I heard the lock on the door click as he shut it behind him.

I looked at Blaise, who sat on one of the inflatable chairs, reading a magazine. I was suddenly furious.

"Why don't you people have any real furniture?"

He stared up at me, confused.

"I don't know. It's always been that way. I never asked."

"Blaise, do you have any idea how weird your family is?"

"If we're so weird, why do you spend all your time over here?"

I folded my arms tightly across my chest, realizing I still had my shirt off, the way Taro liked me best for when we were lying side by side. I put my shirt back on and felt my face steam with tension.

"Why is Taro in the bedroom with your dad's girlfriend?"

"She likes him."

"Does your dad know?"

Blaise had still not managed to lift his eyes from the magazine.

"Sure."

"Do you ever go in there with her?"

"No, she doesn't like me."

"What about his other girlfriends?"

"Sometimes."

He put the magazine down and stood up abruptly.

"Let's go. I'm taking you home."

❊ ❊ ❊

At my grandmother's apartment two days later, I sat in the half-darkness watching as she read from her book of Psalms. There was a permanent twilight in her apartment, so different from the starkness of the brothers' home, with intrusive light reflecting sharply against the white walls and plastic furniture. I thought of my own family's secrets. We mourned my grandfather's death as if he'd died in his sleep when in fact he'd committed suicide by drinking gasoline.

I thought of my mother, who spent her days painting nails yet sometimes went on dates with men who would give her money afterwards. These were details we never spoke of. I decided every family had its secrets, and no sin was more unforgivable than another. I didn't believe Taro had committed a crime. I imagined his mother as crazy, fragile, and jealous of her husband's other lovers. Her sons were innocent.

When I left my grandmother, I went and knocked on the brothers' door. Taro opened the door just a few inches, sliding half of his body out.

"You can go home, Pigeon. We don't think you should come around here anymore."

"I don't understand," I managed.

"We're tired of this routine of you coming over all the time."

I tried to keep my chin from quivering but tears escaped my eyes, burning my cheek, at the mere tone of Taro's voice and his harsh, unfeeling gaze.

He reached his hand out and touched my arm lightly, then pulled it away.

"Don't cry," he told me, making me feel even more childish.

I wanted to tell him how I'd believed in him despite the horrible things I'd heard, defending him in my heart. I decided to go against all my instincts of protection, of swallowing the secrets of our encounters, the gossip I'd heard, compartmentalizing all the parts of my life. I decided to spit them in his face, in one jumble of disillusionment and love.

"I know what they say you did to your mother, and what your father did. I'll never tell anyone about the time I spent with you and what I saw in your home. They say you're a monster, but I thought . . . I thought you were beautiful."

I suddenly thought of his mother, in an eternal sleep. Her silenced heart had found a way to scream through me.

"They say what you did is unforgivable."

He didn't reveal anything in the way he stared back at me. He barely blinked, looking to his feet for a moment and then back at me. He touched my arm again, holding it on my skin much longer this time, inching his finger along my elbow down to my wrist.

"I know what we are in this house," he said, motioning to the half-open door behind him. He still had a foot inside, and a foot in the corridor with me, "and I know that you don't belong here. That's why I want you to leave and never come back. If we see each other on the street, I'll pretend I don't know you."

He drew in his breath and took a step back, so that both feet were inside the apartment, increasing the space between us.

"And the times that I refused to touch you," Taro began, "were not because I didn't want to, it was because I didn't want to ruin you."

He stepped further behind the door.

"If they say I'm a monster, it's because I am."

I could only offer silence. My voice was hidden behind the tears I struggled to restrain. He took a small step toward me, so that he was close enough for me to touch. I wanted to reach for him, but I knew he wouldn't let me.

"I saw goodness in you," I said.

He shook his head as if he pitied me.

"You saw goodness where there was none."

He slid back into the doorway and closed the door before I could say another word. I stood there, staring at the wooden door in front of me, barricading me from the world inside their apartment. I closed my eyes and said one of my grandmother's prayers for Taro and Blaise, and then for all the families with secrets, shames, and unspoken details, praying for all those who are not who they seem to be.

Snow Geese

Pure menace! The red-faced farmer spits
as he watches them glide
in parenthetical descent into his tender winter-
wheat. Unlike higher beings, they can fly,
their incandescent forms invoking snow.
But like us, they mostly eat and shit.
Late-winter sun with nowhere to go
but up, glances at a stand of loblolly, and there—lit,
as if from within, edges ruffling
like summer's blown rose,
or a slick-haired magician reshuffling
his stacked deck, the flickering body flows
in a wide, emphatic arc—
shattery bits of mercury glass alight against the dark.

Alice Lindsay Price, pencil, copyright 2001

Field Notes from Radnor Lake

I. Mountain Bluebird

This bird is the clutched gasp of surprise.
Now, at the edge of the field blooming
with yellow plumes of ragweed,
this bright muscle of blue
knits in and out of leaves,
surprise surprising me
with its breathless question:
is what I see what's in front of me?

II. Yellow-Billed Cuckoo

You warn of storms
with your rapid, harsh rattlings.
Don't we all need a cautioning voice
clucking from the lowest branch
near our feet, or would we rush
the open field before a lightning storm
anyway? I understand why Zeus chose
your elusive body to disguise himself.
He knew I wouldn't resist
stroking your silky feathers
if ever given the chance.
Love: how often it's used to lure us,
to turn oneself against oneself.

III. Northern Cardinal

A child's curiosity begins this bird's life.
She asks, "What's that red one, Mother?"
and learns its name first. Strong curve
of sound at the beginning, lull at the end.
The girl decides her life will be this sound,
beautiful as this bird, but then the disappointment

when she learns how the female colors herself
a ruddy brown and lets out a single,
incessant chirp from the nest, again and again,
telling her mate she's alone, telling her mate
she's doing that angry act of waiting.

IV. Common Grackle

Black, iridescent death, you first
cluck slowly, then raise your voice,
screeching like the back gate's hinge
someone forgot to oil.

I forget about you,
but then you raid the birdseed,
and I, after cursing,
will set out a full pan again
with a new plan to keep you away,
you, this rat of birds,
this hunger of man,
this willfulness to expect change.

V. Ruby-Throated Hummingbird

Love hovers like this
with its thin seam of energy
before it dips and lifts away —
then returns
once we've settled in
to living without it.

The Anatomy of Birds

If ever God's heart was drowning
in fifty gallons of despair, I would mention
the anatomy of birds as a flashlight
to shine through His heavy grief.
Avian Pallium, I would say, and God,
even if lost in the agony of a thousand
thunderstorms, would remember the kindness
of this gentle bone,
how it protects the *Cerebral Cortex*
like hands wrapped around
a small snowball.

God would remember, upon hearing *Anterior
Air Sacs*, how once He took the last
embers of creation to give each bird
a small breath. I would say *Synsacrum*
for the tender way God fused
their *Vertebrae*. I would point
towards a lone crane and whisper
Syrinx, for sparrows barely above
the sleeping trees, *Fovea*.

If ever an ocean of God's teardrops
fell like boulders from a gray-black sky
each of us should recite
bones found in the generous wings
of birds, *Alula* and *Scapula, Humerus*
and *Ulna*. We should tongue the names of each
tiny gland, *Uropygial, Malaclemys,*
our recitation not stopping
until God's swollen heart had risen
from its midnight of sorrow, until God could once more
hear His birds singing, so far in the distance,
even as they fly against His terrible wind.

The New Physics

My father was dead when he came to Napa for a visit.

We carried in his luggage and he sat down to have a slice of Sara's
    cranberry bread.

We drank coffee, he talked about work, and the next day we went for
    a drive along the Mendocino coast.

This isn't the first of my father's *appearances* and Larry's been offering his
    opinion that it has something to do with space/time relativity.

He says my father has an irrational way of understanding the universe
    and has been living for years in four-dimensional reality.

But theories like this only go so far in explaining how my father has been
    waking without the slightest hint of a heartbeat.

For over 15 years he's been disappearing for months returning with nothing
    but missing teeth.

Local papers have speculated that perhaps my father's ability to defy death
    is proof of Penrose's Black Hole theory.

Jim says in 1957 the Many-Worlds Interpretation predicted the possibility
    of someone like my father accomplishing this sort of feat.

Even Bell's Theorem, Jim says, which only recently has been received by
    science, suggests life and death are a matter of perspective.

But when my father came to Napa it was the middle of summer.

We grilled hamburgers in the backyard and opened a bottle of Sonoma
    chardonnay.

That night Cameron and Stacey stopped by sometime after two and once
    again it all came back to subatomic particles and Max Planck and
    for a few moments they shared a heated debate over the supposed
    shortcomings of S Matrix.

160

Come morning Cameron still couldn't let go of the quantum mechanics
involved in von Neumann's disproof of the Distributive Law.

The night before my father left I took him to the cabin at Clear Lake.

As evening came we sat on the pier eating cheese and drinking Red Tails.

Through the silence of conversation I stared into darkness listening for
breaths that wouldn't come.

My father's risen above the failure of his heart to beat and of his blood to
flow.

He's risen above kidney failure and throat cancer and what once seemed
to be the irrefutable laws of science.

And it was like this that my father was dead as he raised his hand like a child
and waved to stars galaxies away and which have been sending
for countless generations these small drops of quiet light.

Manly Johnson, photograph

Meditation in January

From my desk in this room,
only north light through two windows,

I watch the sky transmute, milky blue,
to the gray harbinger of more snow.

One crow traverses, heading I think for protection.
The wind picks up
and whistles through the sashes.

When did I begin to think of myself as old?

✺

I fall back to a house ghostly in shape —
Around it, fields stretch to the tracks
and beyond to the river.

Ark of a house that is no more.
For years as a child I lived there and roamed those fields.

✺

One day as the light was going, I went to the river,
the forbidden river. Bitter winter.
Ice like thinnest lace at the water's edge.

The snow, which had started slowly to fall,
increased and swirled around me

hiding the lights of the house,
then hiding the whole landscape.
But I found my way.

That was the night a child I knew, a boy of seven,
tried a shortcut
to his home and froze under an oak.

✿

Just before dawn the doorway
from my bedroom wears black.
The black is shadow night puts back
                    where light was.

The day is coming up gray beyond the pond,
rising out of night into the light-bloom.

The door to the room beyond this room —
what is, what thing is not quite real,
                            and waits there?

✿

I am hoping for light — a death, easy as this memory:
a sun-blazed field,
Grand Isle on an August afternoon,

the deer stopped at the perimeter
between meadow and woods, reaching to pull down
leaves from the lowest branches into their tender mouths,

there where the sky is knitted to the field
their delicate bodies open to whatever comes.

✿

But bless even the cold moments,
the snowstorm that fell last night
not with heaviness,
            but in the slantwise, wind-driven slurry
            that shifts and slides through day and into night
to fill the river with lessons about erasure,
            each thin flake dissolved into the whole.

Almost Ghazal with Thoughts Toward Spring

Nothing loosens the way a brook loosens from April,
ice hurls up along the edges, block after giant block.

Peepers rev up, mole salamanders breed in vernal pools.
It seems as if the voices of the songbirds all unlock.

A poet I knew lived in a mountain cave, wrote on trees
and sang to the wind. Light's time, his only clock.

Animals have souls also, and trees and blossoms, maybe rain.
Once I thought I saw a soul embedded in a rock.

The dream world is another as real as this. I pass between the two,
as through a membrane, through a line, or arc.

Winter leaves me in a hush, trailing its long scarf of hours. What door
slides back at last, Patricia? Light comes in. No need to knock.

The Gifts of Linnaeus

after Native New England plants named by Carl Linnaeus

What is sacrament if not to take in the names—
      the twinflower for instance he named for himself,
Linnaea Borealis, its fragile bells ringing long past

his brief moment in the world.
      Or smooth sumac for making ink, for spilling
on the page, for keeping what might be lost.

Not for me the altar rail or the intonations
      of the priest. Not the vessel lifted up,
nor the disc like a diatom on the tongue.

No, this is the body—this mountain laurel
      it is forbidden to pick, its blossoms like lights
against the dark woods, or the red mulberry

that failed to survive New England winters—
      someone's dream of silk that didn't come to pass.
And this is the body, the common milkweed's clouds

of blowing across the field and this, too,
      what is left behind—the dried husk. And this
is the body—lobelia whose name fills my mouth.

And this is blood—the wild grapes clinging
      to the wall behind which the traffic
of the interstate rushes with a river-sound—

and this too, high-bush blueberry whose bright
      gems gather a sheen of morning dew, their stain
on my willing tongue.

And here is New England aster, its flowers
      bluer than wine. Eat and drink, here, now,
on this giving earth, these sacraments.

DAN PAGIS

Father

July 18, 2007

"So, Dani'le, you intend to write all this down and to publish it? Write, write, don't be shy. Even if anyone reads this, they
won't believe it. As long as you yourself really believe it."

❁

"You never understood your father," a burly man, one of my
father's partners in cards, said to me, "you never understood him
at all. You look like him, but only from the outside, forgive me for
being so blunt." I get worked up: "And so what? Does he have to
come back to life for me to understand him?" "No, no," says the
cards player, "it is you who have to come back to life. But, if you
forgive me for being so blunt, there isn't much chance of that."

A Dream

This is my father. Deep snows cover him, the whole breadth
of the bed. I (it is me, isn't it?) am sitting by the bed, looking at
him. I am wearing an overcoat and of course have to tear it. So
that's that. But no, he holds out a hand to me, he is alive, he is
full of life-blood, the snows have receded, his body with the large
liver spots (judging by the photographs, he was so good-looking
in his youth) is swelling. "Should I measure your pulse?" I ask
him worriedly. And he, reluctantly: "My pulse? What for?" He is
very red, he is burning. He starts to tell me a story he forgot to tell
me yesterday, about the clerks in his office, will they go on strike
or not. This bores me, but I pretend I am interested: "And so, will
they go on strike?" He is grateful for that, he is exceedingly nice to
me, it is really awful. And I thought that was truly the end of it, but
he will upset me yet, he will be the end of me, as right then he falls
quiet, shrinks, detaches himself from the bed, straight and yellow
as a reed, as a stalk of straw, and floats in the air.

166

Shoes

"And you, Dani'le, for example, you think you were all right? You made my life a misery, God help us, do you hear, ever since you came here. Suddenly I had a son, almost seventeen, a new immigrant, confused, if you get my drift. All my love, if I can put it like that, wanted to come out to you, and never got there. In the beginning all you wanted to talk about was that man from Radutz whom you knew as a child, who stole your rucksack on the way to the ship. You could not stop talking about him and said you would never trust another person. But Tel Aviv charmed you, you wanted to learn Hebrew straightaway, and towards me you showed civility or maybe we should say indifference. Always polite, yes Father, please father, I liked that but I did not really love that if you know what I mean. And like that all the time. Maybe only in the last three or four years, during my last illness, you found a reason to shout at me, because I did not always care to swallow all my pills in the order the doctor prescribed. You shouted and I felt some closeness. You think you spared me by not talking about important things. Did you have to wait for me to die? I am not saying you condescended to me, if that is the right word, but you always remained distant. Alien. For heaven's sake, didn't you know I wanted to take care of you? I did not have any money (you should have chosen yourself a rich father, ha-ha) but we did go to the Youth Immigration people to arrange you a place in a kibbutz (do you remember, we went to an agency in Jerusalem? They charged me five pounds. And then we still had time to visit the Western Wall, they told us it was safe, it was in the spring of '47). In Tel Aviv I was always ready to come with you to arrange things, also when you happened to visit us on Saturdays, in the years when you were anyway in Tel Aviv, when you studied in the Teachers' Seminary. Don't tell me you did not enjoy coming with us to that restaurant on Dizengoff. Why are you laughing, I don't know how to put it, I am not talking about restaurants here."

"Yes, Father, I give you credit for much more than that, you tried in many different ways. Do you remember, one winter, when I came from the kibbutz for a visit. My shoes were heavy with mud, I left them outside the door. And in the morning, a surprise, they stood by the bed black and gleaming: you polished them! You polished my shoes!"

"Don't make a great drama out of that, Dani'le, I always liked to polish things."

The first anniversary

The anniversary of your death. You chose to die on the ninth of Av, the birthday of the Messiah, and you knew that one could make a joke out of this as well. But your suffering was cruel, just like the pangs of the birth of the Messiah, till you were redeemed. I was not at your side then, it was not not my fault, completely by chance, and I came back only for the funeral.

On the ninth of Av there is a fair at this cemetery. Crowds collect around the traders at the gate and buy carnations and cans of juice and plastic memorial candles. On your anniversary, here we stand, we five mourners. In this faithful troop are your wife (I remember now: she is the fourth one) and two of your pensioner friends (it is too far for the others). A year ago we also went to the office and hired the service of the cantor on duty, a Yemenite tired from too many memorial ceremonies. Reluctantly, he dragged himself after us, but when we found the grave, he came to life and trilled beautifully, fervently, in a thin voice. And you laughed, I heard you, you laughed because we organized for you an oriental surprise party.

This year I'd decided: no cantor. We are standing by the tombstone (we were cheated: we paid for a second-rate one and got a third-rate one) and suddenly your wife takes out a coleslaw jar (with the Tnuva sticker still on it), fills it with water from the tap by the pathway and sticks in it the bunch of carnations she bought at the gate. And another surprise: she brandishes a rag and bends down to wash the grave. She scrapes, she rinses. And now it is my turn. I say Kaddish, slowly but in an embarrassed voice. One of your friends remarks behind my back: "I will not force my son to perform any memorial ceremonies for me." But this is not enough for your wife, she mutters, "You should have prayed more."

They turn to go, and I stay with you for a minute. I am glad you did not laugh this time. I was four years old when you left us, and seventeen when I came to you after the war. It is easy to keep the score: how many years? Before and after these years, we lived in the same country, next to each other. And right at the end, by no fault of mine, completely by chance, I was not with you. You came late in life, I came late in death. The score is even, and not even that: who needs it any more. I release you from all your oaths and obligations and from all your self-justifications.

1983

Ever since he died a year ago, Father speaks better Hebrew. He says to me: "I confess, it can be said that I deserted you twice. In, when was it, 1934 (imagine, almost 50 years ago), I immigrated to Palestine and immediately found work in Tel Aviv. I prepared everything for your coming, yours and your mother's. And suddenly she died there and I did not go back immediately to take you with me. I am saying it to you again, because you tend to forget. It was so sudden, Grandmother, your mother's mother, sent me a telegram to Tel Aviv, which I did not want to understand. And anyway I could not come straight away, it was all ships then, not planes, and of course I did not have any money, not much in any case. It is true, four or five years later, in 1939, when I came for a visit, I left you there as well, with Grandfather and Grandmother. They said to me, where are you going to take the child, into sands? into the desert? Even though I told them wonders about Tel Aviv, and there was much to tell! and I agreed to leave you with them. I was not ready for you yet. I was about to wed, as they say, to marry Beba, and I thought—it is not important what I thought, it was in Russian. Who knew then that a World War would erupt and so on? And so you were stuck there in the World War and the Holocaust, yes, you get angry when people use that word, you say people exploit it too much, but now that I am dead, I allow myself to call the baby by its name. Excuse me, I did not mean to make a pun, and we will talk yet about the baby's name, didn't you even change the name your mother and I gave you? Well, and after the war? I even managed to get you a certificate (did I ever tell you that the British were impressed by the case? They were used to children asking for certificates for their parents and not vice versa), and so you even came lawfully, legally, with a British visa, in a normal passenger ship, what was its name? As it happened, they cheated me at the travel agents,' I paid for a place in first class and they stuck you in third. Doesn't matter. And of course you want as always to ask the same question, why didn't I come to meet you in Haifa? And let me give you the same answer, because you tend to forget. No one knew then when the ship was supposed to arrive, there were mines all over the open seas, there was no schedule. They said they would let us know, but even the people of Haifa did not know, to say nothing of the people of Tel Aviv. Suddenly it came and dropped anchor in the port and of course I was not there. And when you found people who gave you a lift to Tel Aviv, true, I was at a cinema with Beba. You tend to remind me of this as if it were a funny story: I come back from a drama at the cinema, and here is a drama at home, a grown-up son falls from the heavens. But you did not have to wait outside, the landlord let you in, treated you to coffee. Till we came. Nu, and afterwards in the Youth Organisation in the kibbutz. It is true that we decided you'd stay there only for a year, till you learnt some Hebrew. A year passed, you were miserable and demanded I take you out of there, to the city, as I promised. I did promise. Where would have I taken you to? Indeed, we lived in a nice area, close to Dizengoff (Did you know he was an uncle of mine? I never asked him for anything, though of course he died early, just a year after I came), but you will remember that we only had the one room, even the kitchen was shared with the landlords. Where would you have stayed, under the bed? By the way, do you know the story about under the bed? A man comes home and finds his wife. . ."

"Father! And why didn't you have anything? A chemical engineer (that is also what you printed on your business cards) with a diploma from France, but here in Israel, random jobs, you worked in a bank for a couple of years, the bank went bankrupt. After that you became an importer of butter (what an idea!) and it went all mouldy while still at sea; you opened a coffee house close to the square, and it failed as well, all this you yourself told me. What else? Importing silk stockings for the rich Arab women in Jaffa. When I arrived, you told me with joy about a permanent job: as an accountant in the leather warehouse of what's his name, in that dark cubbyhole in the south of the city which I somehow managed to visit. The rolls of leather were full of dust (I actually liked their pungent smell). It is only in recent years that you'd had a job that had anything to do with chemistry, yes, yes, I see some significance in that, a vague connection, it is true, in the Standards Directorate, quarter chemist and three-quarters clerk, but then you never took anything completely seriously. You think it is all a gas, you make jokes about everything."

"Don't count that against me," he says. "It is good to make people laugh. Only with you I have always failed. Your sense of humor, let's say it is peculiar, OK, you have no time for that.

You studied in the Teachers' Seminary and became a teacher in a primary school and then in a secondary in Jerusalem and then in the University, and always preoccupied and so ponderous it comes out of the other side. It's not that I am complaining. On the other hand, as they say, better a son be a beggar and honest than a gambler and so on. Do you know the story about the woman and the cards? She complains: 'My son can't play cards!' Her friend says to her, 'But that's good!' and she says, 'But he plays anyway!'"You see, Dani'le, one has to know how to live, as well as how to play."

"And were you to come back to life, would you show me how?"

He thinks for a moment and says calmly, "There is no need, it is simpler like this."

"What's wrong with you?" I scream. "I don't want to be buried here next to you, there is no place, and anyway, Father, there is no time, I must get up and go to work." But now he holds on to me and says with great affection: "Again you worry? What do you mean, no time, you will work everything out, to the very end."

1984

This ninth of Av, the second anniversary of your death, only the two of us mourners remain. Before noon, I come to collect your wife, Annushka. She asks me with concern: "Do you have what you need to say there?" I remembered that in among the books in the living room there was by chance a prayer book, old and falling apart. "I do," I say to her. "Ah, is this the Biblia? " she asks. No end to wonders. "No, no, how do I explain this? Biblia you read, from this you pray."

This time she buys carnations in the shop next to the house, haggles: "Listen, Mr. Azulai, drop the price a little bit, it is for my husband's grave." I blush and give the seller a bill, but she stops me emphatically: "For my husband I buy flowers myself."

The number 92 bus to Holon is crowded, people try to escape the burning sun, and all huddle on the shaded side of the bus. In

Holon they move from side to side, shade changes sides with each turn. I sit in the sun and keep quiet. But Annushka, who holds the bunch of flowers, feels the need to talk: "It is far, you know, but it does not matter, we are not in a hurry." Opposite us, in a seat with its back to the driver, sits a workman in overalls. He remarks: "Right, what is the point of hurrying? They will wait." A minute later I realize that I understood correctly, and indeed he meant the dead. What impudence.

In your cemetery, the ninth of Av fair is in full swing, seething with even more life than last year. The mourners and tradesmen have multiplied prodigiously. As someone with the experience of having already got lost here, I do not rely on the numbers of blocks, but follow the map. Only Annushka hesitates: haven't we just passed block twenty-six, why now block nine? But finally here is block twenty-five, your lot, your row, I make myself a path in the sand among the tombstones, and go to the very end. The grave is nowhere to be seen. Where is it? This time you will not escape me, I came especially, for you, on this special day. I go the full length of the next row, come back to the previous one. Annushka already starts complaining: "Didn't I tell you?" but at that moment you save me. Your grave suddenly appears before my eyes, as if it had always been there, and your name is engraved on it, with the usual thing they write on tombstones, may his soul be bound in the sheaf of life. I call out to her: "This is the place." She hobbles up, opens a plastic basket, and, my goodness, this time again she has brought an empty coleslaw jar. I have already learnt the procedure, I walk up to a tap and fill the jar with water, she sticks in it a bunch of carnations, lowers herself onto the plate of the tomb and washes it.

A cantor is wandering about, stares at us. He's just finished a memorial service in an nearby row and is looking for work: "Would you like a God full of mercy?" "No, no," she says, "No need." And she adds under her breath, "He can ask for a thousand, what do I know. Nu, let us start." I take the little prayer book out of my pocket. As usual, the orphan's Kaddish is printed at the very back of the book, so that ignoramuses like me can easily find it. The letters dance in the blinding sun. *Itgadal veitkadash*, magnified and hallowed be, and everything is finished in half a minute, maybe even less than that. And now what? For we can't go just yet. "You know what," I say to her, "I will read it again." Another half a minute. And what now? Maybe I will find her a psalm. The sun covers the book, I shade the pages with my head and find out that next to the orphan's Kaddish, right on the preceding page, is the blessing for a new moon. Should I say the blessing for a new moon? That might have amused you, but I give up, as usual, put the prayer book back in my pocket and Annushka says, "It is terribly hot, let's go."

And so this time again you've played a trick on me. Only at the very last moment you've flashed the tombstone at me, just like a magician suddenly drawing an unexpected card. What am I complaining about? It was not here that I'd lost you, and it is not here that I will find you. In our long argument you have the last word: it is etched in black letters on the tombstone, right in front of my eyes.

Steps

There was a peculiar rhythm to your gait. A light tap with the heel, and after it a springy tread, optimistic, perhaps somewhat defiant. Light and springy, light and springy. I walk differently, ponderously, purposefully, like now, when every step takes me farther away from your grave. We were complete opposites. You, sweet, superficial and full of joy, and I, insipid and depressed. So, goodbye, this visit in the cemetery has also come to an end, and off I go again, walking energetically down the pathway that leads to the gate.

But what is it I suddenly hear, a light tap with the heel and after it a springy tread, optimistic, perhaps somewhat defiant. Light and springy, light and springy. I start to run. Your steps run after me, with me, in me, your legs are my legs, your death, my death.

Stand still, I command myself. Stand still. It is just me, alone, not you, not you. I admit that we were not complete opposites. I admit that we were very close, closer than I would want to admit, closer than I would have wanted. But the difference between us is clear and will always remain: I wear larger shoes, size 43, while you, as I well remember, wore only size 37.

The end as future

In seven years' time, on the tenth anniversary of your death, Father, at a rare clear hour of Av in Tel Aviv, we shall be sitting opposite each other on the little balcony. And it is as if it overlooks the world from high above, and not from the third floor, and we shall see spread before us the big city, which already for a long time will have become to us alien and strange, crisscrossed with strings of distant beads, amber lights.

And I will quote to you a poem from another land, about a cemetery in another land, but dear to me, I will not be embarrassed, and for the first time ever I will quote a poem to you: *Le vent se lève, on doit tenter de vivre*. You will listen thoughtfully, to honor my memory, but also in amusement, because what has that got to do with anything? But the silence between us will be a silence of acceptance.

A wind and an opposing wind will intermix playfully before our eyes to create a little whirlpool. The curtains behind us will fill out, becoming wide sails, but in the spirit of play. We will not set sail to any place, for we have already arrived, have we not? And you will nod, you will nod in assent.

All Pagis fragments translated from the Hebrew by Michael and Anna Grinfeld

A Great Change

Now
you will see everything
wet and green
this rain wants everything
to do with us
slamming
on the air conditioner

How can I not imitate
the rain in its persistence
don't blame me for being bull-headed
look around you
every mean thought will eventually
settle on a delicate gesture

Who among us
does not understand
those who hurt themselves
paper cuts
the skin that opens
looking for the color beneath
the harm
the piercing flame

You make a wound
in order to go inside

I have been afraid of sinking
in the open air
sometimes you can't tell the difference
between sinking and rising up
the push of sound off
the side of a mountain
or the bottom of the sun
pressing on still water

I amuse myself
planning for the full moon
walking backwards
into all the old dreams

You are horrified at nature
the tiger ripping the jaguar
open
wouldn't you love to reach in
and grab a heart

"Where do the wolves live?" my son asks
His question settles down quietly
on their backs as they travel
down from the mountains
beautiful, slow, stalking steps
like holy words of prayer

You must move down also
into the canyon
sing all the songs
praise every piece of earth
you sink your fist into

Something will be ripped open tonight
as the piercing rain hits everything
to wake it up, to make it clean

You can walk out into
anything fierce
under any dark moon
look up at the silver underbelly of the leaves
they are crying for the storm

Between Us the Sea: Circe's Aubade

> But Odysseus remained true in his heart.
> —*Homer*

He who burns for Ithaca and not for me
  now sails for home and a wife whose deception's
    demurely domestic. What matter if

another nymph with glossy braids
  should sway him from his way?
    Nights when the Aegean is a silver platter of light,

what can I do but fold and unfold my trousseau
  of longing under our bridal canopy,
    old sea nets swathed against the gnats?

Memory, loyal dog, pants at my heels.
  He has his hound, I mine.
    The waves turn their wine-dark pages

and the days advance.
  What I have become or will
    remains unwritten on the palimpsest of my life.

Who knows better than a woman how to turn
  into whatever poor beast the stunned heart wills?
    He was for a time my strong stag striding,

his antlers, wet velvet, moss.
  Now others, mere pets, persist in their pins,
    hide and haunch heavy with tick and flea,

pining for themselves and the men they used to be.
  their minds alone keen as they were before.
    They bray and bleat all night at unnamed stars,

which are neither great nor gallant–only abundant,
  wheeling overhead: no Orion, no hunter, no belt to unbuckle.
    They are nothing to a goddess like me—

a shawl of stars the earth wears
   and the constellation we might have been
      inscribed each moment on the waves before it breaks apart.

Honeymoon in the New World

—for G.C.

We sailed at dawn, newborn colonists
with our rings locked in the safe
and the bright blade of the Caribbean
honing itself on the beach.

For us the world was
wasp-waisted as a bride,
ours alone, in her tourniquet of tulle
with so many layers left to lift.

We came to find paradise
but find others like ourselves,
advancing empires of two along the equator.
Our side of the Huguenot wall:

A kingdom of conch and plantain,
the breadfruit's doughy heart
we cook and call our own.
The island wears her black bracelet of sea

carelessly, a clanging cuff of salt and surf.
Here, sun-scored couples toast
that ancient marriage of convenience —
beauty and brutality.

How else to admire the canebrake's banner
but not the men and mules haunch-high in hunger?

In this month even the moon burns
shadows through the palm leaves,

silvers water in the wells off shore,
and stutters through the shutter across the floor
(a wildfire, and our hearts, timber
about to catch).

My darling, now that we've reached the green shore,
where loss waits like a promise we have made,
what are we to do with this country we carve
late beneath our veil of mosquito netting

when one of us is certain to rule alone at the end?
Even now night steps from her silken gown
of heat and light and approaches without shame,
like a girl who thinks it is enough to be beautiful—

After Reading a Letter

I dwell on virtue, and I long for it,
ever since childhood, since Sir Galahad,
I've wrapped my mind around the strength of ten;
I didn't cheat at games, or lie all day,
I prayed, I said I'd write a song for it,
read Aristotle on the good and bad
and other writers on the lives of men
that gave a hint, a clue, an easy way.

I now have a drawer of maxims, a hill
of beans, a house of cards, a ragged sieve,
a place to put me in my place, a chance
to think again, to mull, to get my fill
of all I thought, of all I would believe,
and smile in wonder at my hangdog glance.

Just After the Snapshot

They dispersed. I held the camera
as a girl her books,
conversations started, loneliness
was now hubbub, the wind moved things
as it would not in the picture.

Poems are not snapshots, nor trophies,
nor time being tricked. Poems
are the moment just after the snapshot,
putting aside the pose, watching life clear,
accepting the real as it hums in the air.

The Last Poem

for Billy Collins

Nobody writes their last poem
knowingly—saying to the gathered
mourners—This is my last poem—
no, it's usually far messier than
that, a medical problem—maybe a
partial stroke—and then the difficult
recovery all that time when writing
poems again seems the furthest thing
from anyone's mind—it would be nice
if there were a flurry of trumpets—
and then the page brings in upon the
silver tray the last white sheet
upon which "the last poem" will be
inscribed—along with the pen or pencil—
and then you can sit down there
with those final thoughts—all the
things you've been putting off
thinking about, or writing about
for fear of hurting this one's feelings
or that one's—surely some exemption
is in effect for this "the last poem"?—
wouldn't you suppose? But it's never
like that—you're in a hurry or
your hemorrhoids hurt, you scribble
a couple quick lines on the back
of a grocery store receipt, using
the CD case from Paul Simon's best
songs as your clipboard, and then
the deer leaps up out of the tall
grass at roadside. What were
those famous lines you wrote?—
hauled off with the blood-soaked
wreck of the car, crushed pop cans,
the CD player with its guts spilled
partway out, still roaring "Graceland,"
the deer's body shoved through the
gaping hole where the windshield
had been and your face.

181

"Bear" Moore

—mauled by a grizzly he'd shot
on the Gila River, 1883

1.
Dreams aside, Geronimo last looked
on the Mogollon range the winter James Moore
claimed a cave on Raw Meat Creek, turned hogs loose
for acorns and denned up, dreaming he'd found
the silver ledge under the waterfall
and every trail hot with bear he tracks
through wind over rock, fur and hair crackling,
treeline a monk's cut flashing blue, steak juice
sunset; he tracks them ghosting through aspen,
and kneeling, sniffs the bed's dirt and moss;
he tracks them through their brush tunnel's
invisible twists, scampering on all fours,
biting knife, blood reading a wildflower's
broken stem, brain baying at what can't be filled in;
emerging briefly in a park of deep gramma grass
yellow and blue daisies, hummingbirds, a stream
winding, he can't recall the time
he wasn't pursued.
                    Alone, he strips and soaks
in the hot springs, listening to snow tick,
the tusk-scarred jaw, skull and pulp-face hidden
by hair and beard, though too tightly stitched
skin twitches, replaying the doll seized and shaken
squeaking: he watches through the window
of his claw-raked chest, his heart feeding, blue-
purplish baby bird hissing like snow.

2.
"Bear" felled, stripped, cut and jointed pines to build
walls and fit beams for roof he piled with boulders:
the mountain mined with dwarf cabin traps
baited with deer's heads and livers for eight-

hundred-pound silvertips, *Ursus Horribilis*,
but once the door drops, he's just another fat
hog-snouted dog roaring, while "Bear" lights pitch
and heats the irons, watching the son-of-a-bitch
slap logs with ham-sized paws and throw his hump-
back up against the roof. "Oh you will eat
a man will you?" "Bear" bangs a dishpan yelling
in those round, stubby ears, migraining skull;
he spears grizz with his Bowie lashed to a pole —
bull-bellows, whines like a hip-broke horse,
fur singed, tusks foaming.
                                        At dawn, "Bear" lies down
and plays possum, chuckling flatly, like someone
who's heard the punch line, then he wools corpse
with teeth and fists, plunging into dog-musk
yanking like a bull-terrier, petting its head,
"I wouldn't have taken these liberties
a few minutes ago." He pulls out claws with pliers;
he hacks off paws for charms, pantomiming
a cuff or two, then walks away, leaving
ruined pelt and all to fly-bloat, gnawers
slithering, juices swelling, popping seams,
carcass dancing again, honied, burning,
wind scattering fur, bones rat-packed; the story
untold — everything but the glory.

Show Me Again Where It Hurts

The day Janet left, we leaned against the wall of the building we'd just eaten lunch inside. We were all leaving soon, but Janet was the first to go, and once she was gone our group, as we knew it, would fall apart. Over beers the night before, Hugh and I had sworn to remain friends. We did it for Janet. We meant it, of course, but neither of us believed it. Janet needed to hear it, though, and so we said it.

Hugh had put his arm around me and given me one of those smiles—the kind of smile that had caused Janet to fall for him in the first place—and said, "Definitely. Definitely. Malcolm, my man, you and me, tomorrow night, right here. We'll drink a beer for Janet."

"Quit," she said. "You're breaking my heart." She was smiling, always smiling, but she was fragile that night. Her hands had been shaking since dinner and even after moving to the bar—the spot that, in only a month, we had dubbed our secret no-no place—she was having to use two hands to bring the beer to her mouth. It was sexy, though, and coy. She had a way of making even her insecurity—on those few instances she slipped and let it show—appear sexy.

Sexy or not, though, I was afraid right then that the evening might turn morose. Words about heartbreak have a way of weighting down a conversation, even if Janet had been smiling when she said them. A table of students next to us broke into laughter, and Janet looked away. Hugh strummed the table, and I—because of the medication and not because I am the crying type—was very close to tears.

It was early yet. I thought the night was over, but Hugh did a final powerful strum then stood up and said, "Vodka. Vodka will liven our spirits." The neighboring table looked over at him, but none of us cared. They couldn't understand a word we said. He disappeared into the next room, leaving Janet and me alone. She had smiled up at him as he said it, but the moment he was gone, she turned her face back toward the table. What a sorry pair we must have seemed to those students.

Her hands were in front of her, smoothing and folding a paper napkin. It was damp from the beer that had been sitting on top of it. I wondered whether I would get to see her cry after all. She began ripping the napkin into nothing, and when she could rip no more, she collected the pieces into one small soft ball and dropped it on the table in front her. I could see her forehead, her eyebrows, the tip of her nose, the suggestion of her eyelashes. She seemed to be having a conversation with herself. She looked at that little white ball; nodded, not at me; then pushed the shreds away, her chin still tucked like some broken bird's wing. She put one finger to each eye, pressed firmly, and looked up at me. She was stunning. She was one of those women whose eyes always looked brighter just before she cried or maybe just after. I wanted to tell her this. Or, more accurately, I wanted to tell her how pretty her eyes looked, but something told me not to. Something told me to stay quiet and that, if I stayed quiet, she might just have something to say to me.

"I miss Carol," was all she said.

"So do I," and I did. Carol and I had been together five years, but those first two weeks in a foreign country had left me more attached than ever.

Hugh came back with vodka, stooping at the doorway from the front room into the back where we were waiting. We toasted to our health and sipped because it was the custom, though we all sipped rather quickly.

"This is the stuff," said Hugh. He took another sip, then smelled the small amount of liquid that was left.

It was dark and close in that little back room. That's why we liked it.

"It reminds me of what I expected from a bar when I was too young to know better," Janet said.

"Exactly," said Hugh. "This is what I fantasized about when I was a kid—low ceilings, dark wood, limited lighting. A patina of character."

The table next to us got up to leave. Soon, it would just be the three of us back there in that room. Hugh reached for the lighter and Janet for the pack of cigarettes. I hadn't smoked in years. It had taken its toll on me to give them up, and I'd been happy without them. But one night early on, Janet had pulled out a pack of cigarettes, and it turned out that both she and Hugh could smoke with a vengeance when drunk without ever craving one during the day. By the end of the month, I was the one buying a pack a day, which is nothing compared to what I used to smoke, but it seemed to signal a turning point in my life—that, and the phone calls from Carol or lack thereof.

But that last night, their body movements were rhythmic with desperation. Janet had a cigarette in her hand before Hugh had gotten the lighter fully off the table. It might have seemed coincidental to Hugh or maybe a sign of some sort—the way their instincts were so well tuned—but it was Janet that night and every night who was so aware of where his hands were and what they were going to do next that there was no room for coincidence. When she saw him go for the lighter, she went for the cigarettes. It was that simple. She got him one as well and they each cradled a white stick in their hands until the conversation about bars and patinas and little-kid fantasies had dwindled. Then Janet put the thing in her mouth and Hugh leaned in toward her to light it, his right hand touching her left, drawing the cigarette and her mouth and her face along with it closer to him. Then he lighted his own and the two of them leaned back in satisfaction at the small touch the opportunity had afforded them. I pulled a cigarette too, but not before Hugh had put the lighter back on the table and I'd taken it safely in my hand.

"I can't believe I never got ice cream," said Janet. "The one thing I could have done to blend in with this country would have been to walk around with an ice cream cone, and I never did it."

"There's always tomorrow," I said, then stopped. "It seems sort of sad—doesn't it?—to fit something like that in so last minute?"

It was possible Hugh wasn't paying attention. It was possible he hadn't even heard our conversation. I suggested we needed more beer, and Janet offered to buy the next round in order to get rid of her excess currency. Hugh said, as she left the table to order, "See you in an hour," because the bartender had been taking forever that night. But Janet hadn't been gone two minutes—not long enough for me to get the courage to ask if he loved her or if he knew that she loved him or, more importantly, whether he was planning on telling his new wife back home about any of this—before she was back, standing in front us with three drafts. Janet had legs to die for.

Hugh choked on the last sip of the beer in front of him and said, "Where'd you come from? You were gone—what?—thirty seconds? This girl can do anything, Malcolm, anything."

She gave us a wink—well, she gave Hugh a wink, but I was
there too and so it was also mine—and said, still standing, lording
above us with that body and those legs and, oh god, those arms,
"He liked me. I charmed him with my confusion. He winked at
me."

"No," said Hugh, shaking his head. "I don't believe it. Not
the surliest bartender in this city."

She was still holding the beers: "He gave me the okay." Then
she mouthed the word a second time for effect, slow, sexy, closing
her eyes deliberately.

I suddenly knew just how she looked in the morning when
Hugh woke up beside her those first couple of weeks. Sleeping
together without sleeping together was how Janet described it before it got too serious to keep talking to me about. And then it got
so serious that it seemed not even they were talking about it until,
by the last night and for at least a few nights before then, they had
stopped sleeping together altogether.

We were friends, but they were more. Not that I was the
third wheel or the odd man out since Carol had been a fourth for
the first two weeks, but I was the one who facilitated those glances,
those long, long glances between the two of them after I'd said
something awkward or rambled on too long about nothing. I'd say
something and then catch them looking at one another and sometimes the look was just that, but other times it stuck and Hugh
would mouth something to her or cock his head and she would
mimic him, all the while the two of them never taking their eyes
off one another, like a pause where nothing mattered—not me, not
their relationships back home. Nothing. Then the conversation
would resume and one of them would turn on with energy and take
the role of entertainer of our little crowd.

Janet used those long arms to reach across the table, placing
Hugh's beer first in front of him, then mine in front of me. Finally,
she took a seat across from the two of us—though more directly
across from Hugh—, slid the third beer in front of her chest and,
lifting the glass, now with only one hand, drank one long fluid
swallow, her elbow never leaving the table. She had incredible
limbs.

She put down her beer and smiled. She seemed calmed by
the trip to the bar, and Hugh, wanting what any grown man would
want—to touch her, to own her, to keep her—, reached his own

sorry arm across the table to move away a lost piece of hair from in front of her eyes and said, "Thanks for the beer." There was the faintest, briefest moment during which she leaned her chin into his hand, blinked slowly, and then, his hand gone back to his side of the table, she tendered one of those stares to which I would never be privy other than as an observer.

I put my head down. I felt sick.

"Hugh," she whispered.

"That's the first time you've ever said my name to me."

"No, it's not."

"Yes."

"Hugh."

Maybe if I hadn't been there.

"You're drunk," was all she could muster.

"Malcolm is drunk. I'm not drunk."

"You're drunk."

"When did you get the upper hand? Why does it feel like you've got the upper hand?"

"It's only fair," she said. "You have it all day long."

"We never got caviar service."

"Don't."

"We didn't go back and see that painting. We never got dressed up, just the two of us."

"Please don't talk about those things. It's too late."

"We never did a midnight boat ride."

"It hurts when you say those things."

"Where does it hurt?"

"Here," she said.

I heard a soft knock, and I imagined her hand on her breast-plate, her fingers spread and shaking.

She said, "You never say these things in the morning when you're sober."

"Where's fun Janet?"

"That's not fair."

"I adore you."

"Stop it."

"I adore you."

"Say it in the morning."

"Why are you so serious?"

My head was on the table, my arms tucked neatly in my lap. They thought I was asleep.

"The difference between you and me," she was saying, "is that I'm the same in the morning and you're not."

"I mean all the things I say." He sounded sober to me. He sounded steady, but what did I know, I was close to drooling and couldn't keep my eyes open. "I just can't live up to them in the morning." There was a pause. I imagined his hand sliding across the table. I think I felt his elbow brush against mine. "I adore you," he said again, this time more quietly.

"And I you," came from across the table.

"Show me again where it hurts."

There were other things we said that night or tried to say, like how Carol asked me earlier over the phone whether I wanted to end things—a comment that each of them had ignored when I said it the first time early on in the evening but also when I tried it out a second time on the slow walk home, probably out of necessity for their own hearts—, but eventually the last beer had been drunk, the last sip of vodka too, and there was nothing to do but go back to the hotel and say goodnight.

Hugh nudged me and I nodded to attention, lifted my head and yawned.

"Is it time?" I said.

"It's time," said Janet, and we walked home, Janet lagging behind by a step or two, each of us all too aware of the pavement and our feet and trying to appear less drunk than we really were.

The problem was that they were the same person—moods, thoughts, mannerisms. They both preferred needing to being needed, which is why there was such panic in them. Hugh was kindest to her when she didn't want it or at least seemed not to need it, and the same went for Janet. The exquisite hours were when we started drinking and the beer drowned out the power struggle as well as the necessary walls of defense they constructed during the day as reminders that they would be going home to different people. Those tender hours when they forgot they were trying to hide their affair and why, and they were in love, and it was a thing of beauty. Even for me, whose own girlfriend was still in love with another man, maybe even still sleeping with him, this thing between Hugh and Janet somehow made it bearable, at least on the good nights, when they seemed to breathe for one another. You might think there's no pleasure in being with two people who forget your existence and fold into one another. But there is. I have

never experienced the intensity they shared that month and probably never will. It was nice to see it played out in front of me for
real, not just in the movies. I think I probably loved them both or
at least their love for each other.

❖ ❖ ❖

Outside the next day, the day she was leaving, there was a
silence. We knew that the moment we moved indoors, the minutes
would move faster. We had an hour. Janet was looking at me, but
her body was turned toward Hugh. I knew I should have left them
alone and I knew Janet wanted to be left alone, but I couldn't do
it. Because it had been us, the three of us, and I was essential for
their affair. Besides, the thought that she was leaving was unbearable to me and even if the one thing she wanted was to be alone
with Hugh, I couldn't give it to her. I was selfish. I still am.

There was a breeze and Janet moved her arms along her
sides to hold down her skirt. We pressed against the wall, Janet in
the middle, letting pedestrians walk by, some of whom we knew,
none of whom we acknowledged. We were waiting.

Hugh said, "We could get Janet ice cream," and Janet said,
yes, instantly, because she was going to say yes to anything Hugh
offered, not because she was a pushover but because she was less
skilled at hiding her heart, beating it down where it needed to be
beaten in order to stay sane. So Janet said yes, all childish and
nervous and crazy, and Hugh said, "Really? I was joking."

She was quiet, but only for a second, because she refused to
be humiliated on her last day, and so said, "Oh. Well, then, I think
I will get ice cream. I think that's what I'll do." I had the idea right
then that if I'd stood close enough, not touching her, I could have
felt her heartbeat coming fast and sick through her skin.

Hugh said, "You're serious? You're getting ice cream?"
There was panic in his voice, and Janet might have regained the
upper hand, but she folded. She said, no, probably not. She didn't
want to eat ice cream alone. And this was when we leaned, three in
a line, against the wall for a second time—the breeze still threaten-
ing to pick up Janet's skirt—in the sorriest sort of silence.

We waited as long as we could before Hugh kicked off the
wall and said again, "Let's get Janet her ice cream. If that's what
she wants, that's what we'll give her," and Janet again said yes

because she knew it was for real this time—that he wouldn't humiliate her twice in such a small amount of time—and I just grinned, and the three of us walked to the vendor, taking our time, strolling as best we could.

"What kind should I get?" She was talking to Hugh.

"It's your ice cream."

She slid open the lid of the vendor's icebox. She nearly didn't have to lean over, her arms were so long.

"This one," she said. "Yes, this one." It seemed to me she wasn't even looking at the ice cream, like if she'd been blindfolded right then and asked what she was holding in her hand, she wouldn't have had a clue.

It was an ice cream sandwich.

They passed the thing back and forth, taking one bite each, Janet keeping her bites small and demure. We were headed in the direction of the hotel again. She offered me a bite but I declined. She was always offering me things. Always asking how my legs felt when we'd walked a long way to a bar or a restaurant. And I was always telling her I was fine.

I started saying all the things Hugh couldn't say. Saying them, if he had said them, would have made it real. They could pretend at least that this hadn't ruined them. "It won't be the same without you," I said. She smiled, lips closed, and gave me only the slightest of glances.

We stopped in front of a church halfway between the ice cream vendor and the hotel. It was Hugh who stopped us. Janet passed what should have been the last bite to him and he took it. He nearly finished it too but something seemed to register and he handed it back. "Last bite is for you," he said.

She took the thing and smiled, eating it without hesitation. She licked her fingers. There was chocolate on her lip. I considered pointing this out to her, but decided against it. She would lick it off soon enough, and it wasn't like it was bad looking.

"You know they modeled this church on St. Peter's," said Hugh. "But I can't see the resemblance. It's so small."

Janet looked at him.

"What?" said Hugh.

"You say that every time we walk by here. Every time."

"Maybe I do."

"You do."

"Did you ever go inside?"

"I did," said Janet. She kicked at the cement, then looked at the sky. "But I'd like to go inside again. I think a church would do me good right now."

She was still holding the ice cream wrapper. There was a messy chocolate coating on the inside. We walked up the steps, and Janet looked around, presumably for a trashcan. There wasn't one. She folded the wrapper in her hand, keeping the chocolate on the inside. Her hands were shaking again. There were no pockets on her skirt and she had no place to put the thing. I considered taking it from her, but again decided not to. It wasn't my place. She was cupping the thing in her palm like a tiny grave. At least it gave her something to do with her hands. She was making me nervous.

We walked three in a line into the belly of that church and stood there, not saying anything. There was nothing left to say. There were other tourists, other Americans, other voyeurs. But there were also actual congregants, real women with real veils, really praying. I watched these women, small and sad.

I looked at Janet. "Will you really come visit us?" I didn't have the heart to say it would just be me, and not Carol, she would be visiting.

"Maybe," she whispered, not turning her head toward me, though earlier in the week she'd been planning a road trip and all the meals we would eat together, all the beers we would drink.

"What will you remember most?" It was Hugh talking. He was whispering, not looking at either of us, the old women in veils still praying in front of us. Janet turned to face him then, turned squarely toward him, her face, her body to him, her back to me. I don't know what her expression was. I don't know if she was holding back tears or if she was already crying or if she was simply mad. She didn't say anything or anything that I could hear. Then she turned away from both of us and headed toward the exit.

Hugh and I followed her all the way to the hotel. I kept thinking she would turn around and say something—a last-minute pithy remark—but she didn't. The breeze had picked up, and she gathered the excess material of her skirt in one hand, holding it fast and hard at her side as she walked in front of us. She looked fragile and a little bit unsteady. Her movements were awkward and disjointed. She walked quickly, and we matched our pace to hers. At the front door of the hotel she stopped, her palm on the handle,

the little piece of trash still clutched in her fist. We waited, the two
of us a few steps down from her. She turned, lording above us one
last time, and said, "Will you two be around for the next twenty
minutes?"

Hugh said, "What time is your taxi?"

"Two." She glanced at her watch, her right hand still on the
door. Hugh climbed a stair. She was still looking at the watch. He
reached out to her, put his hand on her wrist, turned it just slightly.
Neither of them said a thing. They stood there, me watching from
the bottom step, the two of them just looking at the time.

"I'll be in my room," I said. I couldn't stand to watch them
do this to each other, to me. I think I'd finally had enough. Janet
looked at me. I never want a woman to look at me that way again.
I'd broken hearts before and I'd had mine broken, but I'd never
seen a look like that and neither have I seen one since.

She said, "I have to get my bags together. I'll come up and
say goodbye before I leave." She took her wrist back and went
through the main door, then the lobby door, then up the stairs,
without ever turning around.

❖ ❖ ❖

She knocked on my door just before 2:00 p.m. From the
other side, I told her to come in but she didn't. I got off my bed and
opened the door. She looked at me for maybe a half-second, then
moved her eyes away from mine. Her hair was pulled back and her
cheeks were pink and moist. She looked almost regal. She gave me
a nod, still without looking at me, then stepped exactly one step
inside my room and put exactly one arm around my neck, and I
heard a small gasp. Such a small noise for such a tall thing.

I took her in as quickly as I could—that moment, that smell,
that tiny, tiny breath. But then she was gone. She didn't say a
thing. And I closed the door out of respect, but I leaned against it,
my ear hard against the wood, to learn whether she had already
stopped at Hugh's door or was saving him for last. I thought I
heard a pause, but I'm a romantic, and it's more likely that she
just kept walking, trying to keep it together, that little half gulp of
salty breath the most she'd allow herself until she was on the plane
or maybe beyond. I closed my eyes, my forehead still against the
wood, my newest roommate (one of many conference participants

the three of us had shunned over the past four weeks) in the background already asking who was at the door and why they were leaving three days too soon, and I imagined that walk of hers down the four flights to the first floor where her luggage was already waiting and how she was just sitting there, chest heaving, hands shaking again, waiting for the taxi and privacy and the rest of her sorry life to begin.

The only other knock I got that day was from Hugh. I'd spent the afternoon alternating between reading on my back and sleeping on my stomach. My roommate had finally left me alone in order to walk around the city, and I was happy for the empty room. My medication had reacted poorly with beers the night before, and I was still exhausted from a night spent on the toilet with a trashcan in my hands. It was after dinner when Hugh knocked, and when I said come in, I almost expected to hear Janet in her sing-song falsetto say "room service," followed by Hugh's deep laugh, before the two of them kicked open the door. Instead, all I got was Hugh.

He took a seat on my windowsill and picked up the book closest to him and started reading. It was a guidebook. He'd already had a few beers, and it was a minute before he said anything.

"What we have here, Malcolm, my man," he said, his face still in the book, "is a reason to get shitty."

I sat up on my elbows, rested the book I'd been reading on my chest, "Where do you have in mind?"

He flipped through the pages of the guidebook, then read aloud—he had a magnificent voice—, "Belly dancers and good service are par for the course at this hole in the wall . . ." He faltered. "A bender, Malcolm, a bender is in our future." He flipped though another couple pages, paused. "Hell, the secret no-no place. What's the point in trying someplace new with only three nights to go?"

"Secret no-no place," I said and swung my feet off the bed and onto the floor. I picked up a shoe. Within a year, it would be necessary for me to revert to shoes with Velcro rather than laces. I knew the likelihood of my fate even then and so was thankful even then for the ability still to tie my shoes, albeit somewhat clumsily.

My back was to him. Right then, if he'd asked me whether or not I thought she loved him, I would have said yes. If he'd asked whether or not she thought he loved her, I would have said no. If he'd asked whether I thought he'd messed up, whether he should have risked everything by laying it all on the table, I would have said yes to that as well. But if he'd asked what I'd have done in his shoes, I would have told him to fuck himself.

He said, "It sounds funny to say it without her around, doesn't it?" I paused mid-rabbit ear, not forgetting which movement came next but not remembering which cell in my brain I needed in order to make it happen. I dropped the laces. I would have to begin again. He said, "Secret no-no place. It was her expression and we appropriated it. It sounds childish without her in the room."

I glanced over my shoulder. If Carol had still been around, I would have waited until Hugh left the room, and then asked her to tie my shoes for me. It didn't occur to me to ask Hugh.

He was looking at me, his finger marking some inconsequential page in the guidebook. I knew I would never get the conversation from him that I wanted; I would never get him to say aloud that he loved her. I said, "Yes. Childish," then went back to the rabbit ears. Drinking was the only solution. Medication be damned.

Hugh bought the first round and we toasted Janet. It was his idea and I give him credit for that. There are many things I will never give him credit for, but for that, the credit is his. "To Janet," he said. He was sitting in the same spot she'd sat the night before.

"Janet," I said.

We knocked glasses, and I watched over mine as he drank half his beer in the first swallow. He leaned against the wall.

"I'm exhausted," he said. "I need to leave this place." I didn't say anything. I didn't have the energy. "How's Carol?" he said.

"Fine."

"She still balling that other man?"

He was joking.

"Yes," I said.

They had ruined us, Janet and Hugh. It had been too much for Carol. Something in their relationship had reminded her of something not in ours. And she'd had to leave. Not that she was there for the right reason anyway. We'd lied and said she was my wife. Pride had kept me from telling them the real reason I needed her with me, which was that I might relapse any minute and that I was no good at giving myself injections. They would have let her come if we'd told them the truth, probably with less hesitation. But my pride was still a problem then, probably still is.

With the time difference and all, Carol was perhaps waking up in that other man's arms about the time Hugh walked to the bar rail and ordered four more beers.

"I can't drink two more," I said as he approached the table with a beer in each hand, a waitress following him with two more. "It's injection night."

"Only one is for you."

I sat there, not saying anything. The waitress set the beers on the table, and Hugh winked at her. He'd have done it in front of Janet. It didn't mean anything. But I remember wishing right then that I was the fighting type. I remember wishing I could summon the rage I used to feel before I got sick and before I had to inject fluids that encouraged my emotions. I wanted to hit him, and I think he sensed it. We drank, I slowly, he quickly. A song with lyrics we understood came on, and Hugh leaned back and played the table with his fingers. He mouthed the words, picking up his hands and shoulders with exaggerated effect.

It was an act.

I watched, sipping my beer, waiting. He finished the song, drained the second of the three beers still in front of him.

He said, "Listen, I don't get to go home to her." I didn't say anything. I wondered how much he'd mind if I took that last beer after all. "Listen, what should I have done? What could I have done? Do you understand me? It would have ruined my life. Fuck you, man. You think I've ruined hers, but she's ruined mine. Fuck you. You think it doesn't matter to me as much as it matters to her. You want to punch me? Guess what? I want you to punch me but you can't because your fucking hands don't work and that shit you take to make you better makes you weak. Guess what? I'm miserable. Is that better?"

He put his head in his hands. "Hugh," I said. His back heaved just slightly. "Do you know she loves you?" I realized I might be ruining any chance she had with him in the future. "Hugh, do you know she told me she's in love with you? Last night, she was right there, right where you are tonight. You were getting us vodka, probably flirting with one of the waitresses. She was just drunk enough, and she said it. Do you know that? Do you know she's leaving him? Not for you. Not *for* you. But *because* of you. Do you know that? And what did you give her when she left today? What did you say to her? Fuck yourself." It was the beer talking. I could always blame the beer. "Carol's left me. Did you know that? She's left me because she couldn't stand watching the two of you together. Hugh. Are you listening?"

I said his name again, and this time he put up a hand, all five fingers spread out, and all of that hatred seeped out of me. My shoulders felt heavy. He was right; my hands were worthless. I wondered how I was going to give myself a shot when I got home. I would have to wake my roommate — that fucker who had taken Carol's place, that loser whose name I couldn't remember even when I was sober. I would have to wake him up and ask him to put a needle in my ass. But even the hassle of the shot I knew I was too drunk and too clumsy to give myself wasn't enough to wipe away that hand in front of me and the reminder of the two of them the night before and my half-second glimpse into their private world.

We were in the stairwell of the hotel; it was late. We were drunk. Janet suggested the elevator but Hugh said no. My stomach had already started its nauseating spin, and I jogged the steps two at a time. Hugh was mimicking my awkward dash upwards, but Janet was still lagging.

In spite of my stomach, I turned on the landing halfway between the third and fourth floors to say goodnight to her one last time, the ice cream still a thing of the future. I opened my mouth to speak but stopped myself. I had caught one of their clandestine signs. Hugh was behind me a stair or two down, and Janet was in the doorway of the third floor. He had just put up his hand, spread-palmed, and what I thought I saw was Janet mouth the words, "Yes. Five." And it made me happy to think she wouldn't be sleeping alone, not that I understood their need to hide it from me. They thought what they were doing was wrong. I wish I could have convinced them it wasn't. There is no harm in love; there is no wrong, and she loved him. I know that much. I know also that she saw me see that furtive sign and that she didn't care that I knew she would be up on our floor in five minutes, knocking on Hugh's door, her teeth freshly brushed. She had ceased to care for me. Not in a cruel way. With time passing so quickly now, she only had room for Hugh.

The Seine

Every day Paris opens its shutters
to sunlight I dream of Vientiane
and the tin ceilings of the Ha Ha Ha
Cigarette Factory we slept beneath.
Hens pecked in the dooryard
of the Ministry building as we passed,
the French long gone—I pressed
the front of my dress to trap sweat
trickling between my breasts,
the heat like a body over my body
slowly shifting its weight,
the Mekong sluggish and brown,
unlike the Seine, the thatched roofs all
that each house was made of,
with corner posts and sometimes a woven mat
over the dirt, each roof crowned with a TV aerial
catching the signal from Bangkok, each
front stoop a little market for things
we never wanted: soap, large white underpants
from Thailand, colorful junk.
When the sun hits the first slate rooftops of Paris
and makes them shine, it is 3 a.m. in Vientiane.
Bicycles lie beside the roads. Chickens
roost in canopied trees. I will stay here
only a short time and never,
I will never be the same.

Jane

The ending finally comes to me in traffic in Massachusetts.
I'll kill Jane off in a hotel room in Paris in the last chapter.
From then on I'll be on the run. It's all about getting rid
of the body. If this was origami, something unfolding
without any rips or tears, I'd write Jane as a butterfly, or Jane
as ritual, as ceremony, draw Jane with clichés and details
of little consequence—Jane steals the Mona Lisa and runs
down the Champs Elysées dressed in a sundress and dark
glasses. She drives and smokes, each butt lit off the one before until the air
is a house of twinkling ash. Jane always wanted to live in France.
She's a romantic. They love animals and the blues. You can turn
on the TV and watch people arguing about the rights of dogs.
I think even the love lives of mosquitoes are protected by law.
Once, trying to write Jane's last kiss, I crawled in bed with my memories
and pulled them over my head like a hammock netted with flies.
Sometimes you are so full of pain you wish you could leave yourself,
let your voice be stolen. On the radio a woman who speaks to wolves
says she has begun to dream she was more animal than human,
and when she was interrupted for a commercial break,
a white man who had stolen a black man's voice—
the French have no word for this—started singing a song
with so many double meanings only someone who has learned to dream
in French could understand. And suddenly I realize a story
I thought was about murdering a woman is about nothing more
than how you can find yourself on a highway outside of North Adams,
and I feel like the luckiest son of a bitch that I've written my pain
into the hands of a woman who doesn't know she drives around
the French countryside with moments left to live, and me inside of her.

The Truth about Virginia Woolf

After the party we cover the pool,
tarp rolled back, scripts put away.
You call them cannibals, those
who lunch with us all afternoon,
our neighbors who would
not stop eating as they demonstrated
and discussed *Who's Afraid of Virginia Woolf?*
faces hung over plates of starfish and sea
cucumber, as though we didn't
already have enough of the ocean
inside us.

You can dissect these things
until they have no life at all,
Albee's symbols and mixed metaphors,
the silences of those characters like the old
people who sat at the lake when I was a child,
waiting for the ones I knew were dying to die.
How scared I was of those long marriages.
I could not mourn with them as they said goodbye,
filling themselves with beer
and ambrosia salad, their shadows on the hard,

buttery white of the faux basilica marble
that put their steamy faces and beehive
hairdos onto a ship moving through a weird Catholic
afternoon. I thought the word Satan came from sated.
How clear the constellations reflect in the folds
of the tarp we lie on. What can we do but fling
ourselves at the water like this, as though there is
some exhilaration that keeps the un-seaworthy afloat
on a smashed sail, where we will swallow anything
to keep from hearing the voices on the lawn.

The House on Prospect Avenue

The previous owner
had hanged himself
in the garage of our house.
I like to think the day was sunny
with large clouds floating by,
the neighbors working
in their gardens, tying up
tomato plants, and small boys
in shorts headed downtown
for orange popsicles. Through
the elm trees you could hear
music from the riverbank where
teenagers were swimming,
laughing, getting burned.
The house was painted light gray
and had elephant vine on the porch,
geranium plants on the steps.
Just as it is now.
As though no time had passed.
As though no one had ever opened that door.

Havasu Falls, Arizona

And so it was that water fell forever
where naked swimmers part the greenish foam
and swing from leather ropes and dive and jump
along the banks where trails begin and end.

Deep below our world in disarray,
the children of Coyote live, boxed in
by canyon walls and men — the sky
a stamp of blue above their heads.

In spring the floods begin that fill
the trails and wash their homes away — the corn
and melons, squash and beans, the willow trees.
Above the pool the mud still hangs in sheets.

They garden as if they planted hope instead,
the People of Blue Water. And all men hunt,
as well as every dog. The horses and the mules
haul mail and groceries and tourists from Japan.

Each day begins and ends like this. The rain
or sun or something in between. But now we sit
and feel the world above: its heavy burdens
wait and watch like wildcats in the woods.

NEDDA G. DE ANHALT is Vice-President of the Mexico PEN. She is well known throughout Mexico and Latin America as a poet, fiction writer, essayist, film critic, and literary historian. The Spanish versions of the poems in this issue appeared in her book *Cuadernos de Exilio* (Editorial Praxis, 2006).

GUILLERMO ARANGO was born in Cienfuegos, Cuba, and lived and grew up in Asturias, Spain. A university professor, he is a member of the Pen Club of Cuban Writers, and has written several books of poetry in Spanish. His book *Memoria de un pasado inmediato / Remembrance of a Time Just Past*, was published by Linden Press (Princeton, 1992), in a bilingual edition. He also has written plays, essays and film reviews.

CATHY ARDEN's memoir, *My Sister's Picture*, was published by Simon and Schuster, and she is currently at work on a new memoir, *A Million Invisible Hearts*. Her poetry and articles have appeared in various newspapers and journals, including *Paris Review, Fiction International, Glamour, Harper's Bazaar, Newsday Sunday Magazine*, and *The Washington Post*. She is also an actor.

LENA BARTULA has been a visual artist for more than thirty years. Her repertoire includes painting, installation, book arts, and mixed media. She has been published in *Solamente en San Miguel, Zingology, Dream Network Journal, Dry Ground: Writing the Desert Southwest* and *Foreign Ground: Travelers' Tales*. Bartula lives and works both San Miguel de Allende and in Pozos, a neighboring pueblo. Her website is www.lenabartula.com.

ASH BOWEN is co-editor of *Linebreak*. His work has appeared or will appear in *Black Warrior Review, Crab Orchard Review*, and *diode*.

KARA CANDITO is the author of *Taste of Cherry*, winner of the 2008 *Prairie Schooner* Book Prize in poetry and forthcoming from the University of Nebraska Press. Her poems and critical prose have appeared or are forthcoming in *Gulf Coast, Blackbird, Prairie Schooner, Best New Poets 2007*, and *Florida Review*. She has been awarded an Academy of American Poets prize and a scholarship from the Bread Loaf Writers' Conference.

STEVEN COUGHLIN teaches at the University of Idaho. His recent publications include *The New Ohio Review, Free Lunch, The Spoon River Poetry Review*, and *Slate.com*.

MARGARITO CUÉLLAR, poet, essayist, and journalist, lives in Monterrey, Mexico. He is the author of numerous books of poetry and winner of many national and international poetry prizes. His work has been widely published in Latin America and has been translated into various languages, including Bulgarian and Portuguese.

LUCILLE LANG DAY is the author of a children's book and seven poetry collections and chapbooks, most recently *The Book of Answers* and *God of the Jellyfish*. Her work has appeared in magazines and anthologies, including *The Chattahoochee Review*, *The Hudson Review*, *Tar River Poetry*, and *California Poetry: From the Gold Rush to the Present*. She is the founder and director of Scarlet Tanager Books, and the director of the Hall of Health, an interactive children's museum in Berkeley, CA.

LYNN DOIRON's prose and poetry have appeared in various literary magazines and anthologies. She is the recipient of California State University, Sacramento's Dominic J. Bazzanella Awards in fiction and expository prose. Her first book-length collection of poetry, *hand wording*, appeared in 2006. She has worked as an editor on *The American River Literary Review*, and in close association with Constance Warloe, editor of two anthologies of letters (Pocket Books and Story Line Press).

PATRICIA ENGEL is Colombian-American and was raised in New Jersey. She earned her undergraduate degree from New York University and her MFA in Creative Writing from Florida International University. She is the recipient of the 2008 *Boston Review* Fiction Prize. Her fiction has appeared in *Boston Review* and *Driftwood*.

SHELLEY ETTINGER's work is in *Cream City Review*, *Mississippi Review*, *Stone Canoe*, *Mizna*, *failbetter.com* and other journals. She was a Summer 2008 Fellow at the Saltonstall Foundation Arts Colony and a Summer 2007 Fellow at the Lambda Literary Foundation Writers' Retreat. She recently completed her first novel and is now at work on a collection of short fiction. She lives in Queens, NY, and works at New York University.

PATRICIA FARGNOLI, recent New Hampshire Poet Laureate, is the author of six collections of poetry; her latest book, *Duties of the Spirit*, won the 2005 Jane Kenyon Book Award for Outstanding Poetry and was a semifinalist for the Glasgow Book Award. Her first book, *Necessary Light*, won the 1999 May Swenson Award, and her new book, *Then, Something*, is forthcoming from Tupelo Press. Most recently, her poems have appeared in *The Massachussetts Review*, *Salamander*, *Margie*, and *American Poetry Journal*.

MOLLY FISK is an NEA fellow in poetry. Winner of the Dogwood and the Robinson Jeffers Tor House Prizes, she is the author of the poetry collection *Listening to Winter* and a commentator for NPR and community station KVMR. She teaches the on-line workshop poetrybootcamp.com and lives in California's Sierra foothills.

RODNEY GOMEZ lives in Brownsville, Texas, and is an MFA candidate in the new Creative Writing program at the University of Texas—Pan American. His poems have recently appeared in *Denver Quarterly*, *Barrow Street*, *The Literary Review*, *The Pinch*, and *Potomac Review*.

RAFAEL JESÚS GONZÁLEZ has taught at many universities, including Laney College, Oakland, California, where he founded the Department of Mexican and Latin-American Studies. His poetry and academic articles appear in reviews and anthologies in the U.S., Mexico, and abroad; his collection of poems *El Hacedor De Juegos/The Maker of Games* was published by Casa Editorial. In 2003, he was honored by the National Council of Teachers of English and Annenberg CPB for his writing.

JORGE FERNÁNDEZ GRANADOS' latest book is *Principio de incertidumbre* (*The Uncertainty Principle*), which recently won the Carlos Pellicer Prize for 2008. He also won the Aguascalientes Prize in 2000 for *Los hábitos de ceniza* (*The Trappings of Ash*) and the Jaime Sabines Prize in 1995 for his first book, *Resurrección*.

MIGUEL GONZÁLEZ-GERTH is a poet, translator, educator, and editor. He was born in Mexico City in 1926; in 1940 he left Mexico for Texas, making the U.S. his permanent home. He taught at the University of Texas in Austin for over thirty years, specializing in Hispanic literature. He has written numerous critical studies and works of poetry and has been published extensively in anthologies and magazines. He is the translator of *Natural Selection*, the collected works of Uruguayan poet Enrique Fierro.

CONSUELO HERNÁNDEZ, of Colombia, is a poet, literary critic, and professor of Latin American Studies at American University in Washington. Her books include *Alvaro Mutis: Una estética del deterior*; and the poetry collections *Poemas de escombros y ceniza / Poems from Debris and Ashes*, *Manual de peregrina*, *Solo de violín*. *Poemario para músicos y pintores*, and *Voces de la soledad*. She is the author of over forty works on Latin American poetry. Her poetry has been included in numerous anthologies in Latin America, Spain, Canada, and United States.

CHLOË HONUM grew up in Auckland, New Zealand. She is an MFA candidate at the University of Arkansas, where she directs the Writers in the Schools program, and is the 2008 recipient of the Summer Literary Seminars/St. Petersburg Greta Wrolstad Scholarship for Young Poets.

Her work has been published or is forthcoming in *Best New Poets 2008*, *Shenandoah*, and *The Paris Review*.

ANNA SUNSHINE ISON has an MFA from the University of North Carolina at Greensboro. She is currently writing a book about Venezuelan beauty queens, based on research conducted through a Fulbright grant. She has lived in Venezuela and Mexico and currently resides in Ho Chi Minh City, Vietnam.

JENNIFER KEY was the 2006-07 Diane Middlebrook Fellow at the University of Wisconsin. Her writing has appeared in *The Antioch Review*, *The Greensboro Review*, *The Chattahoochee Review*, and other journals. She recently won the Poetry Center of Chicago's Juried Reading Competition and is currently a Visiting Associate Professor at Southern Methodist University.

KATIE KINGSTON is the author of three collections of poetry, *Unwritten Letters*; *El Rio de las Animas Perdidas en Purgatorio*; and *In My Dreams Neruda*. Her awards include the Colorado Council on the Arts Literary Fellowship in Poetry and *Hunger Mountain*'s Ruth Stone Prize. Her poems have been published in *Atlanta Review*, *Great River Review*, *Green Mountains Review*, *Hunger Mountain*, *Margie*, *Puerto del Sol*, *Nimrod*, and *Rattle*. Her website is www.katiekingston.com.

SUSANNE KORT, born in New York, lived for years in Caracas, Venezuela, where she practiced psychotherapy. In 2000, she moved to Mexico, where she practices with the Mexican National Health Service. Her work—poetry, prose, translations—has appeared in *The North American Review*, *Indiana Review*, *Antioch Review*, *Grand Street*, and many other journals, not only in the U.S., but in Canada, the Caribbean, Ireland, and England.

CAROLYN KREITER-FORONDA, Poet Laureate of Virginia from 2006 to 2008, has published five books of poetry and co-edited two poetry anthologies. Her poems have been nominated for four Pushcart Prizes and appear in numerous magazines and journals, including *Nimrod*, *Hispanic Culture Review*, *Prairie Schooner*, *Poet Lore*, *Antioch Review*, and *Anthology of Magazine Verse & Yearbook of American Poetry*. She also works as a visual artist, with paintings widely displayed in solo and group exhibits.

GREG KUZMA has taught poetry writing for forty years at University of Nebraska at Lincoln. His latest book of poems is *All That Is Not Given Is Lost*. His *Early Selected Poems* will be published by Carnegie Mellon University Press.

DANIEL J. LANGTON's first collection of poems, *Querencia*, won the Devine Award for Poetry from the University of Missouri. His most recent book is *The Sonnets*.

LETICIA LUNA was born in Mexico City in 1965. She is the author of *Hora lunar* (1999), *El amante y la espiga* (2003), and *Los días heridos* (2007). English translations of her poems have appeared in *Common Ground Review*, *The Dirty Goat*, *Illuminations*, *Shearsman*, and *Visions International*, among others.

PURA LÓPEZ-COLOMÉ was born in Mexico City, spent part of her childhood in Mérida, Yucatan, and attended high school in the U.S. The author of several books, including *El sueño del cazador, Aurora, Intemperie*, as well as her collected poems, *Música inaudita*, she is the translator into Spanish of works by Seamus Heaney, William Carlos Williams, Gertrude Stein, and others. Her selected poems in English, *No Shelter*, was published in Forrest Gander's translation. Gander is finishing a translation of López-Colomé book, *Santo y seña/Watchword*, which won Mexico's most prestigious poetry prize, the Villaurrutia, in 2007.

RITA MARIA MAGDALENO was born in Augsburg, Germany. The daughter of a Mexican-American father from Aguascalientes, Mexico, and a German mother, she grew up in Marcos de Niza, south-side Phoenix, Arizona. Her publications include *Marlene Dietrich, Rita Hayworth, & My Mother* and *My New Backyard Garden*, a bilingual children's book. Her poems and stories have appeared in such national and international publications as *After Aztlan: Latino Poets of the Nineties; Walking the Twilight: Women Writers of the Southwest;* and *Neueste Chicano Lyrik: New Chicano Poetry.*

FELICIA R. MARTINEZ was born in San Diego, eighteen miles north of the U.S.-Mexico border. Her poetry has appeared in numerous publications including two anthologies — *Cantos al Sexto Sol: An Anthology of Aztlanahuac Writings* and *The Poetry of Peace* — as well as in literary reviews such as *BorderSenses Magazine, Susurrus,* and *Poetry Now*. She holds an MFA in Poetry from Mills College in Oakland.

MICHAEL MCGUIRE, a dramatist, lives in Mexico. His play, *La frontera*, won the $10,000 International Prism Competition. Others of his plays have been produced in New York, Los Angeles, and overseas. His work has appeared in *The Paris Review* and other journals. A book of his stories, *The Ice Forest*, was named one of "the best books of the year" by *Publishers Weekly*.

VALERIE MEJER is a poet, painter, and essayist. Her book, *De Elefante a Elefante*, was awarded the International Award "Gerardo Diego 1966" by the Spanish Government. She is the author of the books of poetry *Geografías de Niebla*, *Esta Novela Azul*, and *Ante el Ojo del Cíclope*. Her poetry has appeared in the anthologies *El Corazón Prestado* and *Antología de Poesía de Tema Prehispánico*. Her poems in English have appeared in *Poetry London*, *Hunger Mountain Review*, and *Translations*. She has translated (in collaboration with E. M. Test) Charles Wright's *Apalaquia/Apalachia* and Pascal Petit's *The Zoo Father/ El Padre Zoológico*, among others.

PILAR MELERO was born in Atotonilco, Durango, Mexico, and moved to Waukesha, Wisconsin, as an adolescent. She is an assistant professor of Spanish, Chicano/Chicana literature, and U.S. Latino/a literature at the University of Wisconsin-Whitewater. She also writes short stories, poetry, and plays. Her creative work has appeared in journals such as *Zona de carga* and *Puentes, revista méxico-chicana de literatura, cultura y arte*. Her academic articles have been published by Arte Público Press and *Revista Identidades*, among others.

PANCHO NÁCAR (1909-1963) was born in Juchitán, Mexico, where the native language of the Zapotecs, Diidxazá, is widely spoken, and where traditions are guarded and kept with zeal and pride. Nácar, along with Macario Matus and Andres Hinestroza, is responsible for developing a modern poetic idiom in the Zapotec language. Nácar, now a legend in Oaxaca is the author of the important book *Ti gueela' nacahuido'* (*A Dark Night*).

DAN PAGIS (1930-86) was born in the Bukovina province of Romania. He spent the years 1941-1944 in concentration camps, rejoining his father in Palestine in 1946, later becoming a professor in medieval Hebrew literature. During his lifetime, Pagis published six books of poetry, a children's book, and many academic books on medieval Hebrew poetry. The collection *Last Poems* and his *Collected Poems* were published posthumously. The prose fragments about his father, some of them written when Pagis was already terminally ill, are taken from *Collected Poems* (HaKibutz HaMeuhad/Mosad Bialik, 1991).

GAIL PECK's first chapbook won the North Carolina Harperprints Award, and her first full-length volume won the *Texas Review* Breakthrough Contest. She has published two chapbooks, *Foreshadow* and *From Terezin*, and a full-length volume, *Thirst*. Her work has appeared in *The Southern Review*, *The Greensboro Review*, *Rattle*, and elsewhere. She was a 2007 finalist for *Nimrod's* 2007 Pablo Neruda Prize for Poetry and a 2008 semi-finalist.

CHARLOTTE PENCE's poetry is forthcoming in *Prairie Schooner, Spoon River Poetry Review, South Carolina Review,* and other journals. She has received the New Millennium Writing Award for Poetry, a poetry fellowship from the Tennessee Arts Commission, and most recently the Libba Moore Gray poetry award. Currently, she is a doctoral candidate at the University of Tennessee and poetry editor for *Grist: The Journal for Writers.*

J. J. PENNA is a musician and poet residing in New Jersey. He received an MFA from Warren Wilson College in 2008 and has held fellowships at the Atlantic Center For the Arts and the Vermont Studio Center. Recent work has appeared in *Brilliant Corners.*

HANNAH PITTARD's stories appear or are forthcoming in *McSweeney's, The Mississippi Review,* StoryQuarterly, *Oxford American, BOMB,* and several other magazines. She is the recipient of the 2006 Amanda Davis Highwire Fiction Award and an honorable mention winner for the 2006 *Atlantic Monthly* Writing Contest. She teaches a fiction writing workshop at the University of Virginia's School of Continuing and Professional Studies.

ELENA PONIATOWSKA rose to international prominence in 1971 with the publication of *La noche de Tlatelolco (Massacre in Mexico).* Poniatowska has published more than three dozen works of fiction and non-fiction and is the recipient of over a dozen national and international literary prizes. She is best known for her novels *Here's to You, Jesusa, Dear Diego,* and *Tinísima. Tlapalería,* a collection of eight short stories from which "Canaries" is taken, was published in 2003. Poniatowska's works have been translated into several languages.

ZARA RAAB's poems and literary journalism appear in *Poetry Flash, Arts & Letters, Eclipse,* and elsewhere, as well as (under her father's name) the *St. Louis Post-Dispatch* and *Humanities.* Her poems are inspired by the rural Northwest, especially California, where her great-great-great-grandparents settled and lived among the Sinkyone and Yahi. She studied at Mills College and the University of Michigan at Ann Arbor.

ANDRÉS RAMÍREZ is a poet and editor born in Tetelcingo, Morelos. He has published three books of poetry, including *Zapping,* from which the Spanish versions of the poems in this issue are taken. He has also appeared in the anthologies *Anuario de poesía mexicana* and *Los mejores poemas mexicanos.* He is the literary director of Random House Mondadori in Mexico City.

JOANNA RAWSON is the author of *Quarry* (Pitt Poetry Series), which won the Associated Writing Program's Prize for Poetry, and the forthcoming collection *Unrest* (Graywolf, Fall 2009). She designs gardens in North-field, Minnesota.

ROBERT RUSSELL's short fiction and poetry have been published in various literary magazines, and included in the anthologies *Poetry Slam: The Competitive Art of Performance Poetry* and *From Page to Stage and Back Again*. He has published a spoken-word stereo cassette tape, *Jungle of Roses*, and a chapbook, *Witness*. He has taught workshops at the University of Wisconsin, the National Poetry Slam, and the Universidad Autonoma de Chihuahua, Mexico, and participated in the Semanas de Poesía de San Miguel de Allende, 2003-2009.

ANTHONY SEIDMAN's poetry and translations have been published in numerous journals, including *Bitter Oleander*, *Iron Horse Literary Review*, *Border Senses*, and *La Jornada*, Mexico's major newspaper. His books include *Where Thirsts Intersect* (The Bitter Oleander Press) and the new *Combustions*, available from March Street Press.

PEDRO SERRANO, born in Montreal, studied at the University of Mexico and at the University of London. He has published five books of poems, including *Desplazamientos* and *Nueces*. With Carlos López Beltrán, he edited and translated *La generación del cordero* (*The Lamb Generation*), a bilingual anthology of contemporary British poetry, and a collection of the Irish poet Matthew Sweeney. His poems have appeared in *Modern Poetry in Translation*, *Verse*, *Sirena*, *Reversible Monuments*, and *Connecting Lines*. He teaches Poetry and Translation at the University of Mexico.

JOHN SPAULDING is a clinical psychologist and poet who currently teaching at Pima College in Tucson, Arizona. He has published three poetry titles and one cookbook. His latest book of poetry, *The White Train*, was a National Poetry Series winner in 2003. His work has appeared in *The Atlantic Monthly*, *Boston Review*, *APR*, *The Iowa Review*, *Prairie Schooner*, *Poetry*, and other literary journals.

JOHN SUROWIECKI, a Pablo Neruda Prize winner, recently won the Poetry Foundation's Pegasus Award for verse drama. His play, *My Nose and Me (A TragedyLite or TragiDelight in 33 Scenes)*, was performed at the 2008 AWP convention in New York, the University of Connecticut, and the Chicago Shakespeare Theater. In addition, *Tapeworm Comics: A Graphic Poem in Celebration of the Adolescent Imagination*, a poem in comic book format, is scheduled for publication in 2009 by Ugly Duckling Presse.

RAWDON TOMLINSON has taught writing for many years, most recently at the University of Colorado at Denver. The poem in this issue is from an unpublished manuscript called *Apacheria Tableaux*, which is the sequel to an earlier book, *Geronimo After Kas-ki-yeh: Poems* (2007).

MARÍA DE LOURDES VICTORIA's short stories and children's books have been the recipients of numerous awards. Her first novel, *Les Dejo el Mar* (Ediciones B, 2005), was finalist for the Mariposa Book Award (best Spanish novel) and took third place for Best Historical Novel. A short story was recently published in the anthology *Traspasando Fronteras* (Almería, Spain, 2008). She is co-owner of House of Writers, an online Spanish literary academy.

PATRICIA CAMPUZANO VOLPE was born in Monterrey, Mexico. She moved to the U.S. at nineteen to continue her studies. Aside from writing, she dedicates herself to the practice of Chinese medicine and the study of history, religion, and ethics. She recently moved to San Miguel de Allende with the intention of not only returning to her native country but also, perhaps, to her native tongue.

ANDREA L. WATSON's poetry has appeared in *Poet, RUNES, The Comstock Review, Ekphrasis, Room of One's Own, International Poetry Review,* and *The Dublin Quarterly,* among others. Her show, *Braided Lives: A Collaboration Between Artists and Poets,* was inaugurated by the Taos Institute of Arts in 2003 and has traveled to San Francisco, Denver, and Berkeley. She is co-editor of *HeartLodge: Honoring the House of the Poet.*

ELLEN WISE received her BFA from Virginia Commonwealth University and her MA from Washington College. Five of her poems have been set as a song cycle by American classical composer Adolphus Hailstork. *Ventriloquist Acts of God,* the collaborative work, has been performed widely, including at the Kennedy Center, Washington, DC. Her work has recently appeared or is forthcoming in *Beltway Poetry Quarterly, POEM,* and *Schuylkill Valley Journal of the Arts.*

ERACLIO ZEPEDA was born in Tuxtia Gutierrez, Mexico in 1937. He has published over a dozen books of fiction, poetry and criticism. In 1982 his *Andando el tiempo (As Time Goes By)* won the prestigious Xavier Villaurrutia Prize in the short story category.

Andrés Ramírez

Dan Bellm has published three books of poetry: *Practice*, named one of the Top Ten Poetry Books of 2008 by the *Virginia Quarterly Review*; *One Hand on the Wheel*; and *Buried Treasure*, winner of the Poetry Society of America's DiCastagnola Award and the Cleveland State University Poetry Center Prize. His translations of poetry and fiction from Spanish and French have appeared in *American Poetry Review*, *Poetry Northwest*, *Kenyon Review*, *Two Lines*, *Literary Imagination*, and numerous anthologies.

María Victoria

Wendy Call is the 2009 Distinguished Northwest Writer in Residence for Nonfiction at Seattle University. She teaches creative writing at Pacific Lutheran University and Seattle's Richard Hugo House. She is co-editor of *Telling True Stories: A Nonfiction Writers' Guide* (Plume/Penguin, 2007). Her narrative nonfiction book-in-progress, *No Word for Welcome*, explores the intersection between economic globalization and village life in southern Mexico. Her website is www.wendycall.com.

Consuelo Hernández

Maureen Contreni was born in Indiana and has lived in Venezuela and Brazil. She will receive her JD from The University of Maryland in May 2009 and looks forward to practicing immigration law.

Pura López Colomé

Forrest Gander is the author of many books of poems, translations, and prose, most recently *Eye Against Eye* (poems) and the novel *As a Friend*, both from New Directions. He has edited several anthologies of poems in translation and individual books by Mexican and Latin American writers, most recently *Firefly Under the Tongue: Selected Poems of Coral Bracho*.

Dan Pagis

Anna Grinfeld was born in the USSR and grew up in Israel. She has a PhD in Russian History from the University of Paris VIII and is now at the Department of Near Eastern Languages and Civilizations at Harvard. With Michael Grinfeld, she won the Hebrew-to-English Webber translation prize of Oxford University for their translation of a portion of Meir Shalev's *Roman Rusi*. She has also translated A. Neher's *Le Puits de l'Exil* from French into Hebrew.

Dan Pagis

Michael Grinfeld, also born in the USSR and raised in Israel, is in the Department of Mathematics at the University of Strathclyde in Glasgow, UK. With Anna Grinfeld, he won the Hebrew-to-English Webber translation prize of Oxford University for their translation of a portion of Meir Shalev's *Roman Rusi*. He is finishing a translation from Portuguese into English of a book of poems by

Jose Jorge Letria, *Olivro branco de melancolia*.

Elena
Poniatowska

GEORGE HENSON, a native of Sapulpa, Oklahoma, is a Spanish lecturer at Southern Methodist University in Dallas. A graduate of the University of Oklahoma and Middlebury College, he is currently completing a PhD in literary and translation studies at the University of Texas at Dallas. "The Canaries" is one of eight stories from the collection he is translating, *Tlapalería*.

Leticia Luna

TOSHIYA KAMEI is the translator of *The Curse of Eve and Other Stories* (2008) by Liliana Blum and *La Canasta: An Anthology of Latin American Women Poets* (2008), as well as selected works by Leticia Luna. Other translations have appeared in *Fairy Tale Review*, *Metamorphoses*, *Words Without Borders*, and elsewhere.

Pedro Serrano

KATIE KINGSTON: Please see Katie Kingston's entry in the "About the Authors" section.

Nedda G.
de Anhalt

GEORGE PETTY is the author and editor of books on hiking for the New York–New Jersey Trail Conference. His poems have appeared in the 1991 collection of prize-winning poems published by The Deep South Writers Conference, in *Black River Review*, *Water-Stone*, *Two-Rivers Review*, and *Solo*, and have aired on NPR. His latest publication is a chapbook titled *Boulder Field*, a finalist in the 2004 poetry competition sponsored by Finishing Line Press of Georgetown, Kentucky.

Pancho Nácar

ANTHONY SEIDMAN: Please see Anthony Seidman's entry in the "About the Authors" section.

Jorge Fernández
Granados

JOHN OLIVER SIMON's most recent book of poems is *Caminante* (Creative Arts, 2002). He was awarded an NEA Literature Fellowship in Translation in 2001 for his work with Chilean poet Gonzalo Rojas. Green Integer Press published *From the Lightning*, a volume of his Rojas translations, in 2008. He is the Artistic Director of Poetry Inside Out, a translation-in-the-schools program sponsored by the Center for the Art of Translation.

Margarito
Cuéllar

STEVEN J. STEWART was awarded a 2005 Literature Fellowship for Translation by the NEA. His book of translations of Spanish poet Rafael Pérez Estrada, *Devoured by the Moon*, was a finalist for the 2005 PEN-USA translation award. His book of the selected microfictions of Argentinean writer Ana María Shua will be published by the University of Nebraska Press in 2009.

Eraclio Zepeda

DAVID UNGER is a Guatemalan-born writer who has translated fourteen books of poetry and fiction. His novel, *Life in the Damn Tropics* (University of Wisconsin Press, 2004), has been published in Spanish and Chinese translation.

Valerie Mejer   C. D. WRIGHT's most recent collection is *Rising, Falling, Hovering* (Copper Canyon Press, 2008). She is on the faculty at Brown Univerity and lives outside Providence.

Valerie Mejer   A.S. ZELMAN-DÖRING is the 2008 first prize winner of the Glascock Poetry Prize. Her poetry and translation have appeared or are forthcoming in *The Oxford Magazine, LIT Magazine, The Indy, The Brown Literary Review, The Saint Ann's Review*, and *The Western Humanities Review*, among others. She studied at Brown University, and Saint Edmund Hall, Oxford, and is currently enrolled in the Masters Program in Poetry at Columbia University.

NICK CARTER is a fourth-grade math teacher at Remington Elementary school in Tulsa. He, along with three hundred students and teachers, participated in a celebration of Frederick Remington's birthday organized by Maxine Richards, during which the work in this issue was produced.

DAVID CASAS was born in Ojinaga, Chihuahua, Mexico, and grew up in Chihuahua City. He began his career as a photographer in 1987 and has been part of several collections and solo exhibitions. His website is www.davitciphoto.com.

GERALD COURNOYER is a member of the Oglala Sioux tribe from Marty, South Dakota. In 2004 he received an MFA in Painting from the University of Oklahoma. He has worked as the coordinator and painting instructor for the Oscar Howe Summer Art Institute sponsored by the University of South Dakota and as an instructor at the University of Oklahoma. He has exhibited work in group and solo exhibitions, including several solo shows in New Mexico, South Dakota, Texas, Oklahoma and Shanghai, China. He is represented in Tulsa by M. A. Doran Gallery.

MANLY JOHNSON is a poet, teacher, and visual artist. He was *Nimrod*'s poetry editor for many years. His latest volume of poems, *Holding on to What Is: New & Selected Poems*, has recently been published.

SAM JOYNER's work has been selected for numerous exhibitions, receiving various awards, including First Place Best of Show at the 1995 Lawton Arts Festival and juror's awards in the 1998 and 1999 Tulsa International Mayfest. He is the Chair of the *Nimrod* Advisory Board.

HARLEY MANHART, photographer, is the former Associate Director of the Arts and Humanities Council of Tulsa. She now lives in Taos, NM.

MATT MITCHELL, an artist now living in Sante Fe, NM, is known for his brightly colored monotypes. The yellow warblers featured on the cover of this issue are part of a series of monotypes with pastel and colored pencil that approach each bird's personality with rich color saturation. He is represented in Tulsa by Joseph Gierek Fine Art.

ALICE LINDSAY PRICE, poet, painter, and naturalist, is the author of *Cranes: The Noblest Flyer* and *Swans of the World*. She lives in Tulsa. The drawings on pages 72, 127, 137, and 156 were also used in *Cranes: The Noblest Flyers*, La Alameda Press, Albuquerque, 2001.

MICHELLE FIRMENT REID is a painter and poet who now resides in Tulsa. She was raised in Europe, then moved to Washington D.C., where she received a BFA from The Corcoran College of Art & Design. Her current work incorporates lyrical handwriting within the painting as vanishing commentary. She is represented in Tulsa by M.A. Doran Gallery.

FRANCISCO TOLEDO, a Zapotec, was born in the Oaxaca region of Mexico. The etchings in this issue are from *Trece Maneras de Mirar um Mirlo,* a portfolio including ten drypoints published in 1981 by Galeria Arvil, Mexico City, and also appeared in *Nimrod*'s *Latin American Voices* issue of 1983. He has exhibited in galleries in Mexico, Europe, and South and North America. He was recently awarded the Right Livelihood Award for "devoting himself and his art to the protection and enhancement of the heritage, enviroment and community life of his native Oaxaca."

MARK WEISS, an ophthalmologist in Tulsa, Oklahoma, is an award-winning photographer.

JAMES H. YOUNG, a former university president now living in Arkansas, is an award-winning writer, poet, and widely collected documentary/fine art photographer. Young is a ministerial graduate of the Pecos Benedictine Monastery's ecumenical school for spiritual directors. A cofounder of the Arkansas Metaphysical Society, he is an ardent student of spirituality. His website is www.creationspirit.net.

Nimrod International Journal

The *Nimrod* Literary Awards
Founded by Ruth G. Hardman
The Katherine Anne Porter Prize for Fiction
& *The Pablo Neruda Prize for Poetry*

First Prize: $2,000   Second Prize: $1,000

Postmark Deadline: April 30 of each year

No previously published works or works accepted for publication elsewhere. Author's name must not appear on the manuscript. Include a cover sheet containing major title and subtitles, author's name, full address, phone & email address. "Contest Entry" should be clearly indicated on both the outer envelope and the cover sheet. Manuscripts will not be returned. Entrants must have a US address by October of each year. Work must be in English or translated into English by the original author. *Nimrod* retains the right to publish any submission. Include SASE for results. The results will also be posted on *Nimrod*'s Web site in June: www.utulsa.edu/nimrod.   Poetry: 3-10 pages. Fiction: one short story, no more than 7,500 words.

Entry Fee: Each entry must be accompanied by a $20 fee. $20 includes both entry fee & a one-year subscription (2 issues).

– –

To subscribe to *Nimrod*:
Please fill out this form and send it with your check.

$18.50 for 1 year, 2 issues (outside USA, $20)
$32 for 2 years, 4 issues (outside USA, $38)

Name _____
Address _____
City_____ State _____ ZIP _____
Country_____

For more information, to submit, and to subscribe:
Nimrod Literary Awards
The University of Tulsa, 800 S. Tucker Dr., Tulsa, OK 74104
918-631-3080   nimrod@utulsa.edu   www.utulsa.edu/nimrod

218

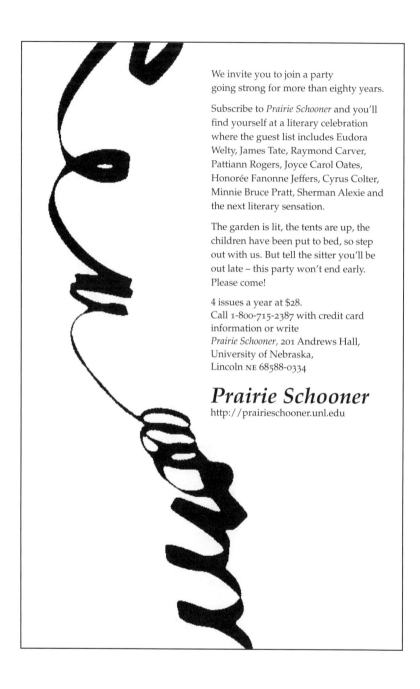